Voices of

GEORDIE
CHILDHOOD

GROWING UP IN TYNE AND WEAR

Voices of
GEORDIE CHILDHOOD

GROWING UP IN TYNE AND WEAR

JO BATH

This one's for Esther,
growing up Geordie.

First published 2014

The History Press
The Mill, Brimscombe Port
Stroud, Gloucestershire, GL5 2QG
www.thehistorypress.co.uk

© Jo Bath, 2014

The right of Jo Bath to be identified as the Author
of this work has been asserted in accordance with the
Copyright, Designs and Patents Act 1988.

British Library Cataloguing in Publication Data.
A catalogue record for this book is available from the British Library.

ISBN 978 0 7509 5656 7

Typesetting and origination by The History Press
Printed in Great Britain

Contents

Introduction

For over forty years now, Beamish Museum has been gathering and recording oral histories – interviews in which people from all walks of life, from right across the North East recount their memories of times long past. Without the museum's dedication to the collection and preservation of interviews, photographs and archive material of North Eastern life sustained for over forty years, this book could not have been written. Within the archives are stories from Victorian and Edwardian times, from the Depression and two world wars, told by housewives, farmers, miners, teachers and more.

The collection includes many tales of growing up in Tyne and Wear and some of the most striking of these have been brought together to form this book. Here you will see all the variety, hardships and comforts of life in Tyne and Wear, in an age now rapidly passing from memory. The earliest stories take us back to the Victorian era, the most recent to the 1950s.

All of the interviews used here are currently within the Beamish audio collection. Some did not start there, though, and special thanks go to all those others who made recordings and donated them to the collection. Several of the voices here were preserved by Newcastle Library or come from the West Newcastle Local Studies collection. Another great source was the recordings made by Jim McGurn in the early 1980s. His book *Tyneside Memories*, which contains seven first-hand accounts of life before the Second World War, is highly recommended.

For reasons of space and clarity it has been necessary to edit some of the memories presented here, but I have done this with as light a hand as possible, to allow the interviewees' own personal stories to shine through. Still, some things are lost in the transcription of the spoken interview to the written book, not least of which is the distinctive accent of the region. A list of the interviewees, together with their dates and places of birth, can be found at the back of the book. All the interviews can be listened to at the Regional Resource Centre, Beamish Museum.

The stories told here are accompanied by photographs drawn from the archives of Beamish Museum, and Newcastle Library Local Studies, two extensive and fascinating collections of images. Selections can be found at collections.beamish.org.uk and the Newcastle Library photostream on www.flickr.com, respectively.

All images in the book are drawn from the Beamish Museum archive with the exception of those duly credited.

Jo Bath, 2014

One

Our Family

*W*hatever the circumstances, a story of Geordie childhood is almost always a story which starts with life in the bosom of the family – parents ready with a hot meal or sharp word, and brothers and sisters sharing the same bed. In the close-knit communities of Tyneside, aunts, uncles and cousins were often just down the street.

Mam and Dad

For most children, a parent's word was law, even if some of them, like Jim G.'s father, made a joke of it. He had lost an eye on the Somme, around twenty years before, and Jim remembers: 'He used to get sort of an eye sent by the government once a year, and he used to place the old ones all over the house. He'd say, "It doesn't matter what part of the house you go into, I've got my eye on you!"'

Some kept their children on the straight and narrow by words, others by deeds. Ethel B., who grew up in South Shields in the 1890s, says, 'I never knew my father lift his hand – his word was enough. That's how you were brought up in those days. Mother used to stop your pocket money and wouldn't let you go out.' Joe G. remembers 'if any of the neighbours gave you a clip you didn't dare tell your father, because he'd give you another clip.'

But of course, parents were there for the fun bits of life too. Mrs A., who was born in 1898, says, 'I had a marvellous dad. He would buy a pound of sweets to share out on the Sunday morning. He used to take us on the horse and trap for a ride in the country in summer, up the Barrack Road. It was lovely country up there then, there was no houses.' In the 1930s E.M.'s mother 'used to make writing books for us to write in. We had paper blinds, and every now and then she used to replace them, and she would cut those up and stitch the corner, and we would use those as notebooks.'

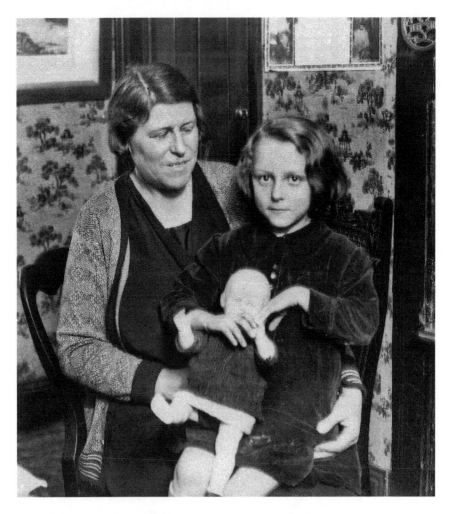

Mrs Jane Moffatt and her adopted daughter Betty at their home in Percy Street, Wallsend.

And parents could influence a child's interests. In the 1930s, Joseph D.'s father (a second generation Italian living in Gateshead) had an accordion. 'When we were children, he used to play at night. It used to wake us up when we were in bed. We would come and sit on the stairs and listen.' Joseph was only 8 when he began to play the accordion himself.

Brothers and Sisters

One hundred years ago, the average family nationally had 3.5 children (compared to 1.7 children today) and in the North East it was higher still![1] Most children had at least one baby brother or sister, and often several in quick succession. One Edwardian New Year's Eve, Mrs A.'s brother was born. The doctor came 'in a sledge, drawn by a horse with big bells around its ears, to bring him into the world. It was snowing, the thickest snow, when he was born. He was fat when he was born. They had to cut the little gowns up with scissors, he was so fat. But he was lovely.'

Mary remembers the delight of finally getting a little sister: 'Early in the morning, Agnes come in and said, "Come on, come on, get up, we've got a new baby" and I said, "You're only telling fibs." She said, "Get up, we've got a new baby and it's a girl" – and after having three lads, a girl was something special. But I didn't believe her. Anyway I got up and sure enough, there was a new baby, and a girl. Marvellous.' She remembers a midwife coming to help out. 'Mrs Richardson was sitting by the fire, washing the baby in an enamel bowl on a stool. I remember saying to her, "Eeh, isn't he little?" She said, "Not as little as you were, I could have popped you in a pint pot."' Elsie D. was a Gateshead midwife in the 1940s, and remembers that youngsters were often fascinated by the new arrival: 'You'd bath the baby, and all the other children would be sitting round and watching. "Can we watch the baby being bathed?"'

Christenings were big family events. Norman A. remembered confidently telling the minister that his little brother was named Tommy,

---

1   This statistic comes from 'A Century of Change – trends in UK statistics since 1900', House of Commons Research Paper, 1999.

after an errand boy he was fond of. '[The vicar] was just going to christen him and he said, "Is it going to be Arthur Thomas or Thomas Arthur?" And my mother said, "Oh, there's no Thomas in it!" And he said, "Well Norman said that!" I was in so much trouble!'

Where large families lived in small flats or houses – and most did, especially in industrial districts – it was often a struggle to fit everybody in.

Miss J.S. in her baby chair, Sunderland (*c.* 1918).

Percy B. lived in a two-roomed cottage near Newburn. His grandmother and parents slept downstairs in the kitchen, while he and his brother and sister 'climbed up the ladder, up the wall in the corner. There was no steps up in them houses.'

Children commonly slept end to end. In 1930s Jarrow, Robert M. shared a bed with his wife and his youngest child, while his five other children shared a second bed. There was a similar situation in Tom H.'s home in 1920s Hetton-le-Hole. 'There was my mam, me and my brother, my two sisters. Us kids used to sleep in one bed, and mam had a bed of her own, and my grandma and grandda and Uncle Joe all slept in the bedroom.' And John H.'s family 'had two bedrooms and to tell you the truth, I still cannot understand how we all fitted in. Downstairs in the kitchen, there was what we called a dez bed, or desk bed, a double-doored piece of furniture and inside there was a bed which had folded back in, and you pulled this out and the clothes and the mattress was inside as well. I often slept three in a bed.'

Older children, especially girls, landed the job of looking after their little brothers and sisters, whether they wanted it or not.

A boy pulls a primitive pram, made from a fruit box, along the Quayside area of Newcastle.

Mrs B.C. was only three when she was given duties with the new baby: 'Mother used to say, "Now lie down on the mat pet and get the baby to sleep." So I used to lie down with the baby on the mat you know. And she used to say, "And don't put your hand on her" – that would be

In Quality Row, Byker, in 1912, three children pose for Fred Halliday, an *Evening Mail* photographer. (Courtesy of Newcastle Libraries Local Studies collection)

in case I put my hand on her face.' Mary remembers: 'You used to have to rock the cradle till the bairn went to sleep. Many a time we wanted to go out to play, and the bairn wouldn't go straight to sleep. Someone would come and call for you, so you'd rock the cradle so hard from side to side, the poor bairn was knocked about, bumped on one side and then the other. The strange thing was, the babies used to seem to like it. We used to sing the lullabies we learned at school, like Golden Slumbers Kiss your Eyes, to try to get the bairn to sleep quick.'

For Ethel A., who grew up in Newcastle in the 1910s, being the eldest child in a big family meant she didn't have much time for herself, especially after her mother contracted rheumatic fever. 'When my mother had the youngest one, Kitty, I had to bring her up as a mother would. She had to sleep with me, I fed her and everything. I was never a good scholar because I had to always mind the baby instead of going to school.' At the same time, and just down the road, Mrs E.C., whose mother died when she was 8, formed a strong bond with her two sisters. 'Wherever I went, I always had Maggie by the hand. I was always pulling her socks up for her. We were like mothers to each other, us three girls. We were left without our mother but we looked after each other.'

No matter how careful you were, in a time before antibiotics small children were vulnerable to many potentially lethal diseases. In 1910, over one in ten newborns died before they were even a year old, and many more didn't reach adulthood. Mary and her brother had pneumonia at the same time – she recovered, but her brother died. The disease returned to the family in 1922, when she was 10, and took her sister Hilda. 'She had a little cart thing with a horse's head on the front, on a string. My mother was pushing it out with her foot, and pulling it in, and little Hilda was sitting watching it running, too ill to make a lot of fuss about it, just watching it. Jim was a very affectionate bairn, and when Hilda died he put his arms around mother's neck and said, "Don't cry mum, cos Hilda's getting married."'

— *Aunties, Uncles, Grandmas and Grandpas* —

It wasn't uncommon to find several sets of relatives living on the same street, living close to where they had been brought up, perhaps following in a family trade or industry. Horsley H. was an only child, but he probably didn't get lonely – in the 1920s, his own family, his grandparents, several aunts and uncles, and fourteen cousins lived in houses sharing a single Byker back lane!

Still, elderly relatives could be something of a mystery. Mr O., who was born in Newcastle in 1906, says, 'In those days the old ladies used to say they were really old when they were 55 or 60. They just retired and lay themselves on the sofa, put a lace cap over their head and they were just grannies from that day onward. I always remember my grandmother like that.' Even in the 1930s, Robert W.'s great aunts seemed to have stepped out of a novel. 'I remember as a young boy being taken up to this gas-lit street, and I had to be very, very correct. I was sat in one corner and given a scrapbook with etchings of the old *London Illustrated News* to keep me amused. Little boys had to be seen but not heard. My great aunts were very, very old fashioned. They were the sort of women that you thought were on castors because they seemed to have no feet – everything was covered by those voluminous skirts.'

It's easy to forget how much life expectancy has increased in the last century, and how that has affected family life. In 1901, only 15 per cent of the population were over 50. One result was that more children were left with one or no parents. When this happened, other members of the family often stepped in. When Mrs E.C.'s mother died, her father asked his sister for help. 'She come to be like our mother, after our mother died. At the beginning she come and lived in our house, for about three year, then she got married and father married someone else. So we just went with her. My father didn't desert us, he used to come across from Gateshead to see us. He was a good dad, many a one would have forgot about us but he never did. My aunt was good to us as well, and her husband Johnny was like a dad to us really.'

When Ted C.'s mother died, 'the problem was who was going to look after the baby, and someone didn't wait for a democratic decision to be made, they stole me and took me off to [relatives in] Boldon. Then they

Studio portrait of a Newcastle grandmother and granddaughter.

brought me back the next day, I'm supposed to have cried all the way there, cried all night and cried all the way back. Eventually my father's only sister, she took me and she brought me to Jarrow.' Ethel R. was brought up by her grandparents in 1900s Gateshead. 'I was the eldest grandchild, and in those days it was very familiar for a child's mother to leave the baby with her mother. I don't know why. But I did see my parents. I remember my father used to come up every Sunday morning, but I wasn't a scrap concerned about that.'

Things were a lot tougher for bairns left without a family at all. Minnie B.'s husband's mother died in around 1912, when he was only 11. Soon afterwards, he came home from school to find his father had sold the house and moved away! He told her later that 'he was living in coalhouses and washhouses. One morning the man upstairs came down for a pail of water and he saw him running from the washhouse to the coalhouse and he asked him what he was doing there. He says, "I'm sleeping here." He says, "Have you no home?" He says, "No," and they took him in and he was in with them until he was married.' As a young man he became blind, and the doctors blamed this on the time he'd spent sleeping rough as a child.

Luckier children were catered for within the system, but their experience could still be a troubled one. Mary Br. was adopted in 1907, when she was 5. 'On the first day I sat on a chair and waited all day for my sister to come take me home, but she never came. I found when I had to go to bed that I had to stay there. They were very kind to me, but very stern. I was told that the less I was seen the better. I just used to sit and wait; I didn't have any life at all. I wasn't allowed to go out much, and the less they saw of me the more they liked me.' Another alternative was the children's home. These institutions have a reputation as very harsh places to grow up, which was undoubtedly deserved in some cases. But George F. enjoyed his stay at the Cottage Home in Ponteland in the 1920s. 'It was a good life. There were so many children in each house, and a foster mother and father who done all the cooking. They had two ploughs and about four horses and we used to do all our own gardens, and grow all our own stuff – turnips, cabbage, tateys – and make all our own bread.'

Bothersome Birds

The final member of many households was a pet. Miss J.S. had an unusual present one Christmas. 'Mother managed to get a kitten. I used to have my Christmas presents put in a pillowcase, hung up at the end of my bed. I don't think mother got any sleep that night, she waited for me to go to sleep, so that she could put the kitten in the sugar bag on top of the pillowcase.' She named it Santa Clausabel.

Horsley H.'s cousin 'once swapped a rabbit for a parrot, a grey Amazonian one. I remember there was consternation in the house once, because the parrot had got out and pulled all the leaves off my gran's special aspidistra. They've got a strong beak, parrots! So the Amazon grey had to go!'

Destroying an aspidistra was bad enough, but in Mary's house, the birds ruled the roost. Her father 'had the house full of white birds. He had these birdcages ranged round the walls, and you weren't allowed to put the

A couple of men look at the caged birds at a Wallsend budgerigar show.

gason for fear of poisoning the birds. And you weren't allowed to put your hat and coat on in the kitchen, in case it frightened the birds. They used to take the skylarks, and they used to have song contests. And we used to make the lark food ourselves, with pea meal, and eggs, and suet. We used to grate it, mix it all up with your fingers and cook it in the oven and stir it up with a big spoon till it was nice and brown. It would come out like brown crumbs. It used to smell lovely; we used to fancy eating it ourselves. On the Sunday morning the birds had their bath. Everything had to stop when the birds had their bath, because father wouldn't have them frightened.'

Two

Life at Home

Doing the Chores

Before mains electricity and central heating, before washing machines and flush toilets, keeping house was a time-consuming job. Most women stayed at home and kept the family going, as cooks, cleaners, nurses, teachers, seamstresses and even accountants. But there was still plenty of work to go around. Children began to help out as soon as they were old enough to copy. In Gateshead in the 1930s, a toddling Elizabeth M. 'used to sweep the back lane from the top to the bottom, I was noted for it! That was just me, taking after my mum.' But helping out wasn't just for girls, as Tom H. says, 'You all had your chores. There was nothing sissified about anything. All the boys I knew did the same. You got the coal in for your mam, and took the ashes out.'

In a pre-health and safety era, children were often allowed into hazardous industrial environments, and taking bait – lunch – into engineering works and shipyards for hungry relatives was a common chore. For boys, this was a good introduction to the place where, chances were, they would start work in a few years' time. Before the First World War, Mrs E.C.'s father was a stoker for a Scotswood gasworks, and she remembers 'going with his can of tea and sandwiches. We would sit on the coal and he would give us a drink of tea out of his can lid.' A generation later, Margaret R. took lunch to her father at Wallsend slipway, in a red spotted handkerchief with four knots in the corners. She hated the shipyard, but says, 'I think half the school used to get out at quarter to twelve, to get out there with their dinners.' Gordon R.'s grandfather, a Sunderland forgeman, had a special trick he would show Gordon at bait time. 'If there was a hardboiled

A young Newcastle girl plays with a coal scuttle (*c.* 1940).

egg in his bait that grandmother had sent down, he would put it on a block and start working. This dirty great hammer would come flying down, and he could stop it so it just touched the egg but it wouldn't break it.'

Back at home, the tasks were never ending. Winifred W. particularly hated cleaning brass stair rods. In 1910s Gateshead, Rebecca B. had to wash and tidy the kitchen, and fill up the paraffin lamps every morning, while her brothers chopped sticks and carried coal. Over the river, Mary Br. would 'clean the knives and forks, and the shoes. My uncle took a size twelve, and I used to grumble terrible. I had an awful job getting them clean.'

Clippy and proggy mats – carefully crafted fabric floor coverings which could be found in nearly every house – were a long time in the making. Mary says, 'Your mother used to nearly always have a mat on the frames, and if you didn't go out you used to get a progger pushed in your hand. Mother used to say, "If you're not going out, you might as well put a few clippings in the mat", so of course we were glad to go out, to get out of the way.'

A rather more enjoyable piece of home decorating happened every Christmas. Into the 1920s the favourite decoration at home was not the tree but the 'mistletoe', as Mary recalls: 'My mother used to make lovely mistletoes with the two hoops from butter barrels. She used to cover them with newspapers to give them a bit of thickness, and then she used to fold the tissue paper, and wind it around, so it was all fluffy and nice. And you used to put one hoop through the other, crossways, and then put all the decorations on, the sugar mice and sugar watches and those sort of things'. Mrs E.A. of South Shields also made paper chains. 'My mother used to cut the tissue paper and make paste for us. We used to all sit round and paste the chains, and mother used to put them up.' But all this decoration did make for a fire hazard, as Billie C. says, 'All we had was the gas mantle hanging from the ceiling and [the butter hoop mistletoe] used to hang so close to the gas mantle, and it was all like coloured tissue paper around and little glass toys. They were very femmer[2] – if you put your finger through them, they used to break. You had to be very careful with them.'

---

2   A North Eastern dialect term meaning 'fragile'.

A girl in clogs carries a bait tin.

Water and Power

The biggest job of the week was probably the washing. Spending the day agitating clothes in a tub, with a poss stick, was back-breaking and repetitive labour. Young Margaret R. helped her mother in their Willington Quay backyard. 'In the corner was a big mangle, and there was a great big poss tub with two poss sticks. I used to dread that, because when it was heavy clothes, two of you had to do it – as one went up the other went down. I always thought my fingers were going to get caught, up and down, up and down. And remember there was no soap powder in those days, it was all blocks of that blue mottled soap. Oh, it was horrible.' Elizabeth K. was only 12 when her mother died in 1921, and she was left keeping house. 'I used to have to stand on a stool to poss, and my Dad used to poss. The sweat was pouring down. Imagine me on a stool, a big wooden poss tub, with a big wooden poss stick – but I had to do my best.'

The poss tub could be used for washing dishes as well, and Dorothy S.'s brother Billy once started possing without checking what was in the tub, with predictable consequences! Possing usually happened in the backyard because that – or the alley behind it – was where the water came from. In John H.'s yard in Gateshead there was a basin and two buckets on a barrel, one for clean water and the other for dirty. He says, 'You washed yourself in this basin and when you'd finished washing yourself you emptied the water into the dirty water bucket. And the person who used the last of the fresh water in the fresh water bucket, it was his or her bounden duty to take that bucket and fill it with fresh water and bring it back full. There was hell on earth if somebody didn't fill the bucket again after they'd emptied it.'

With indoor plumbing a rarity, most children made regular trips to an outdoor 'netty'. Percy B. remembers: 'You went out across the yard in the snow and everything, you tripped across there sometimes in your shirt tail.' Bath water, too, had to be brought in from an outside tap, and heated up in the oven ready to go in a tin bath. Edwardian girls Nancy L. and her sister 'had to have our necks washed and scrubbed. We didn't have a bathroom, just the tin bath. Somebody said to my mother, "What soap do you use for your family?" And mother says,

"Watson's Matchless Cleansing Carbolic, or the Co-op White Windsor."
That was a bit dearer.[3] She says, "The first gets the cleanest water."
That was true, because all the water had to be carried up and down
stairs from the backyard.'

A young girl fills a bucket from a communal water supply on a dark staircase on
Church Stairs, Liddell Street, North Shields, in the 1930s. A few years later this
staircase no longer existed, destroyed in pre-war slum clearance.

---

3 Watson's Matchless Cleanser was a carbolic soap

   patented in the 1890s and made in Leeds.

A young Gateshead boy stands on a chair beside a table with a washbowl and towel on it (*c.* 1908).

But there were exceptions. In the 1920s Miss J.S.'s father created his own plumbing system. 'He had this extraordinary boiler with one tap connecting it to the hot water tap, and you got water heated at the time. I was ashamed of this contraption – I never wanted my school friends to go into the bathroom! After you had a bath, you turned on the tap from the cold basin, which filled up with the tube, and of course you had to remember to turn it off when it was full. If you left it running, it literally came down the stairs!'

Before mains electricity, and sometimes even after it, light came from fragile oil lamps or gas lights. In the 1890s, in Elizabeth N.'s Gateshead home, 'My mother never used to light the big lamp when we were playing about. She just used to light the little one in the chimney piece, for fear we would upset the other one.' Bedrooms, in particular, remained the domain of candlelight. Joseph F.'s earliest memory, from the 1900s, is of sitting in bed playing with shadows by candlelight, his two brothers 'making rabbits and all different things with their hands, and I would be laughing.'

Food and Drink

Over the last hundred years, people's eating habits have changed a lot. A modern child might not think much of Mr P.J.'s diet in the 1920s. 'Generally we had roast meat on a Sunday, cold meat on Monday, and some kind of hash, Irish stew or Lancashire hotpot on Tuesday. On the other days there might be mincemeat, rabbit or fish. On Saturdays we often had corned beef or tinned salmon. We had quite a lot of milk puddings, sago, rice and, my favourite, semolina. Tinned fruit and custard was a Sunday treat.'

The easiest way to feed a large family on a shoestring was to cook stews and soups. Gordon R. remembers shopping for his widowed mother. 'You'd go down the greengrocers, "penn'orth of potstuff, please Mrs Thompson", and she'd give you a leek, a small turnip, and a cabbage. Three carrots and couple of onions, and that was your potstuff for an old penny, and that was the basis of your soup. Even in the hardest of times, when people were really on the bottom, you went into the houses and there was a big fire on, and a pan on.' And that pan was often offered around: 'I know my grandmother made soup, in a great big black pan, and we used to take a jug down for Mrs So-and-So, and somebody else, they always shared you know' recalls Horsely H.

Meat was usually added to these meals, and no part of the animal was wasted. Mr C.R. remembers that 'our main staple food was sheep head broth. We used to even buy the lights – that was the lungs,

The interior of No. 20 North Street, North Shields, 1933. As well as a bed and fireplace, the room has a table with crockery and a washing bowl.

you know – and beast heart was a luxury.' Another Edwardian child, Mrs E.A., grew up on black pudding and oxtails. And in the 1880s Mrs B.C.'s mother would buy 'four penn'orth of liver, two penn'orth of suet and half a pound of skirt and kidney, that was for dad's pudding.[4] And mam and us, we ate the liver 'til it was finished. We got lovely dinners with it.'

John H. came from a large Gateshead family. His favourite dish was a herring inside a stotty cake, made by his mam. Unusually, his unemployed father also helped out. 'One after another as the family got up, my dad had their breakfast of bacon and eggs ready for them, and I was the last one. My breakfast consisted of bacon skin. The whole frying pan was full of bacon skins, nicely fried hard.'

Most women were expert bakers, turning their hand not just to bread, but a range of other meals. In the 1890s, Ethel B.'s mother made 'currant bread, all sorts of beautiful cakes, rice loaf, seed loaf, all good.'

---

4   Skirt is a cut of beef made from the diaphragm – one of the tougher, cheaper cuts.

Mrs E.A.'s mother got up every morning to make stotty cake and do the washing before the children went to school. Girls often had to help out, too. Mrs A. remembers 'I learned to bake when I was 8. My mother was poorly, so she told me what to do – the flour, the water, all the instructions. It was like concrete when I finished it!'

Even Christmas dinner was quite different from the modern feast. Turkey was a luxury until after the Second World War, and the table centrepiece was goose, rabbit, or whatever other meat was available. Mrs E.A. remembers her mother making Christmas pudding. 'We all had to have a stir, and they used to be boiled and boiled and boiled. And she used to make her own ginger wine, and Christmas cake, and rice cake. It used to be really nice. We used to have to sit and peel the almonds.' In the mid-1880s, Mrs B.C. of Hebburn was invited every year into the house of a nearby engineer on Christmas Eve. Here, she said, 'There'd be two pounds of the best raisins, and she put that on his plate. She used to pour some rum over them and then she used to light them. First time we went we daredn't touch them you know, we were frightened. But when we did touch them we didn't half touch them!' This sounds like Snapdragon, a game that dates back to the sixteenth century, in which children risked burning their hands and mouths by snatching and eating raisins doused in burning alcohol. It was extremely popular in the Victorian period and is mentioned in Dickens' *Pickwick Papers* (1836).

One thing hasn't changed though: children's love of sweets. In 1920s Newcastle, George F. could put even the smallest sums of pocket money to good use. 'We could go to two shops and spend a farthing at one place and a farthing at another. We could buy a big lump of toffee, maybe a bag of cinder toffee, mainly sugar and treacle. It was rubbish but it pleased us all right.' Dorothy S. would also split her penny, buying 'a big black bullet for a farthing and a farthing's worth of taffy. When you were a kiddie and you got a penny you were over the moon.' Nan L. preferred to buy 'sherbet dabs and "Virginia tobacco" – it was coconut rolled in cocoa, I think.' Even wartime rationing was not enough to dent enthusiasm. Harry W. says, 'You had your two ounces ration, and it's surprising how far you can make a Milky Bar go with a razor blade, cutting it up into very, very thin slices!'

Two children look into a sweetshop window (*c.* 1932).

Rationing went far beyond sweets, and ingenuity became more important than ever. Jean W. of Byker 'had whale meat, that was quite nice, and we had tripe fried with breadcrumbs like schnitzel. And the biggest luxury I can remember, when the Americans come into the war, was spam and beetroot sandwiches, it was just like heaven. And dried eggs had just come in from America and nobody liked them, and then someone showed how to use them properly. I thought they were marvellous, these scrambled eggs.' It was still easy to get hold of potatoes, so they became a staple – mashed, and flavoured with anything from sardines to banana essence or cocoa!

Miss J. S. on her father's Sunderland allotment, *c.* 1921.

Life was a bit easier if you could grow your own. Fortunately many families, especially in the pit villages, were already keeping an allotment or vegetable garden. As well as growing fruit and veg, some people kept chickens, rabbits, pigs or ducks. Percy B. was roped into helping in the family's huge garden. 'I always fed the hens down the bottom of the garden. Hens and the pigs and that was in there, they got slops out of the kitchen and people used to bring peelings to you, that hadn't a pig. And then me father killed a pig when it was killing time. It hung up on a hook in the corner and it was cured and you got it for your breakfast, you cut a cleave off for your breakfast on a morning.'

While they were a part of the domestic economy, animals could also be a source of fun. In around 1910, Richard C.'s mother bred ducks in a Wallsend backyard. 'When they were old enough, I got an old mat and stuffed it down the sink in the backyard and turned the tap on, and filled the yard with about two or three inches of water. I let the ducks swim about. But I soon had to stop that, because the dampness would have got into the house if I'd kept it up!' Peg H. remembers the sad demise of one duck, which had clearly become a pet to the children. 'The Ashworths used to have a few hens and one duck, called it Martha, and this duck used to follow you to school and you used to have to turn round and shoo it back. And it must have been during the war, when you couldn't get meat, and rationing ... Poor Martha the duck, Mr Ashworth had the duck for the Christmas dinner.'

————— *In Sickness and in Health* —————

Mothers' care was the first line of defence against illness – and their first tactic was usually a laxative or purgative, whether you needed it or not. In 1930s Gateshead, Elizabeth M.'s mother 'used to give us sulphur and treacle every Friday night, and that was supposed to be for your bowels. One thing she used to give us which again, I hated, was Virol. My brother and I had a pact. He loved it, so he used to eat mine!'[5]

---

5   Virol was marketed as 'a preparation of bone-marrow –
    an ideal fat food for children and invalids'.

Mr P.J. remembers: 'every year my mother would make what she called Spring Medicine – lemonade containing some bitter tasting purgative, probably Epsom Salts – and we all had to drink a glass a day until it was finished. If as a child I was at all unwell, castor oil or syrup of figs was threatened at once.' When Margaret R. was ill with a cold, her mother would 'bring the oven shelves out of the coal oven, and wrap a towel round, and put it on the bed before you went in.'

Home remedies were very important because, up until the creation of the National Health Service in 1948, the doctor would have to be paid for, either directly or through a health insurance scheme. Joe G. says, 'We couldn't afford the doctor, so we couldn't afford to be ill. Never once was I at the doctor. I had bronchitis at the age of two. I believe one of the neighbours, Mrs Dalrymple, saved my life, with camphorated oil – she knew what to do.' Such women, knowledgeable in nursing care and home remedies, provided a vital service. In her corner of Gateshead, John H.'s mother would be called out if someone was thought to have bronchitis. 'We had rock salt, which was very, very coarse salt. When the salt was hot enough in the oven, it was put into the canvas bags, and we used to run along to the house where my mother was in attendance, and give her the hot bags.'

Sometimes though, the doctor was needed. Joan W. had rheumatic fever during the Second World War, and remembers: 'My mam paid two and six each time the doctor came to see me, which must have been very hard. I was in bed for about three month, and it was bottles of medicine, horrible.' Even operations happened at home. Mr P.J. had his tonsils removed on a table in his bedroom. 'My face was covered with a cone. The anaesthetic at that time was chloroform. My father insisted on being present, fainted and had to be carried out.'

Of course, a few problems could not be dealt with at home. If you couldn't deal with troublesome teeth yourself – for instance, tying a string to the offending tooth and yanking it out – then a visit to the dentist was in the offing. Mrs C. was lucky having parents willing and able to take him to visit the dentist when at the age of 3 she developed an abscess. 'I had to have an injection; I had to have the tooth out. He was very kind, he held my hand. He didn't wear a white coat, they didn't in those days, and he said all you have to do is keep your mouth

A group of children carry an enormous toothbrush at a Health Day held in Washington, 29 June 1939.

wide open and I'm going to put this in your mouth and you won't feel anything till we get this nasty tooth away.' Of course, the availability of opium must have helped. To treat her swollen face, Mrs C. 'took poppy heads in a basin with hot water and made a sort of liquid with it, and bathed the place with it, and as you did this you sprinkled in chamomile flowers.'

Mr P.J. had a less happy experience. 'Some incompetence on the part of our dentist led to an abscess and the loss of a front upper tooth. He made a plate with one tooth to fill the gap. As it did not fit properly he persuaded my mother to let him file the front teeth underneath down till it did. After that we went to a dentist in Bayswater Road, Jesmond, he worked in a gas-lit room and his drilling machine was driven by a treadle by one of his feet.'

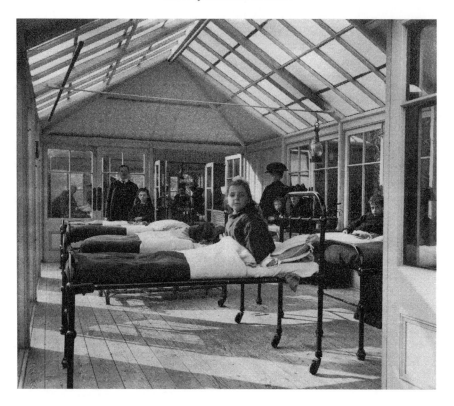

Inside Fleming Memorial Hospital, Jesmond, 1930. (Courtesy of Newcastle Libraries Local Studies collection)

Epidemic disease was much more feared, and much more dangerous, than today and covered carts were used to carry away suspected sufferers to isolation hospitals. Oddly this could be a blessing in disguise, as Jarrow lad Ted C. discovered during the smallpox epidemic of 1926. 'The lads were just stripped down to the buff and went in front of the doctor, and if you had a few spots on your body you were going to be taken away. A lot of us were sent away, including me. We were taken down to Whiteleas isolation hospital in South Shields and there I stayed for three weeks. I stayed quite healthy. It was the only holiday I ever had as a kid, three weeks in springtime.'[6]

---

6   Whiteleas Hospital was run as a smallpox isolation hospital
    by the North East Durham Joint Smallpox Hospital Board
    from 1908 until the NHS took it over in 1948.

Ella G. was less fortunate in her stay at Windy Nook hospital in 1914, aged 5. 'They thought I had pneumonia and the poultices were red hot, made of linseed and castor oil. And it burned all the skin off my side.' In 1925, 8-year-old Mr P.J. also visited hospital, suffering with a mastoid infection. 'My parents were not allowed to visit me at all and I was very homesick. We had bread and dripping for breakfast, which I remember liking, and I had to drink a glass of Cascada Sagrada every night. It tasted horrible.' [7]

Even the professionals were at times forced to improvise. Mrs C.'s sister had problems with her legs from her birth onward. Eventually an army doctor from Fenham barracks came to their North Shields home to advise: 'He recommended special boots to be made, stiffened with copper wire. Well, apparently copper wire was illegal to have during this particular part of the [First World] War, an essential armament type thing. He said she had to have them, and suggested that when she had them she have her legs bandaged on top in case it was seen. They were put on as soon as she awakened in the morning, and she certainly could walk much better.'

7   Cascada Sagrada is made from the dried bark of the American Cascara
    Buckthorn, and has been used as a strong laxative for centuries.

Three

Toys and Games

Making Your Own Entertainment

Most forms of entertainment which so entrance modern children were not available to their great-grandparents – television, though first broadcast in 1936, wasn't commonplace until the 1950s; computer games and iPods were far in the future. In the 1920s even radio was in its infancy. Mary was about 10 when her father made a crystal radio. 'They were just coming out, but he'd managed to get a blueprint from somewhere and he made this crystal set. He used to spend hours with the headphones on, tuning in and tuning in, then he would say, "Oh, I can hear a piano." Then the headphones had to be passed around, everybody had to have a little listen. One night my father sat Jim on the table, and put the headphones on him, and said, "Can you hear anything, son?" He says "Yes, I can hear sausages frying ..." My mother was busy frying sausages for their supper!'

Mostly though, technology wasn't going to entertain you – you had to do it for yourself. Boys and girls enjoyed books and comics, though usually different titles. In the 1920s Miss J.S. spent some of her pocket money on *Little Folks* magazine. Collinson B., in the late 1930s and early 1940s, read 'the *Rover*, the *Wizard* – those comics, they had no pictures in them, page after page of column after column, close print. And we swapped them. It never occurred to us to read comics with pictures in,

Boy poses with a *Say When* comic.

those were for kids. We'd left behind the *Beano* and the *Dandy*, *Lord Snooty* and his pals, *Desperate Dan, Pansy Potter*, and *Radio Fun*, those were for little kids.'

Wartime comics were a lifeline for Harry W. when he was evacuated from Sunderland to North Yorkshire. 'My treasures were the *Knockout* and the *Beano* comics, and the *Adventure*. If they were ordered before war started, you could still get them. My father sent them out to me when I was evacuated, wrapped in brown paper, brown sticky paper. It used to be exciting, it used to take about half an hour to get your comics unwrapped.'

Although reading and games like ludo and snakes and ladders were popular with girls and boys, girls' toys and boys' toys were usually quite different. When Sunderland girl Miss J.S.'s father had a windfall at Christmas, she got a Hornby train set. 'Each time I went out of the room, when I came back again, there was another bit, either track, or level crossing, or signal box.' (Perhaps Dad wanted a train set of his own!)[8] But John T.'s father, a Gateshead tinsmith, was being more conventional when he made John a fort, and his sister a dolls' house.

Few little girls had an elaborate dolls' house like Miss J.S. It was a magnificent Georgian-style three-storey house 'with lovely toys in it – miniature cups and saucers, and a tea set made out of fish-bone, the most extraordinary thing.' In Edwardian times you could buy a much more modest version from the Marks and Spencer Penny Bazaar in the Grainger Market. Mrs E.C. recalls: 'You'd buy a box of dolls' furniture for a penny, but they were stuck with glue to the bottom of the box. You couldn't take them out the box or they would break.'

Nearly every girl had a doll. Mrs E.S. of Sunderland remembers that 'At Christmas, there was an advert in the paper for a nice big doll, and my mother said to me "Would you like it?" When I got up on the Christmas morning, it was a big cloth doll and filled with sawdust. It was beautifully dressed, my mother had dressed it.' But when Mrs E.C.'s elder

---

8   Although she remembers it as being a lottery win, this was long before the
    National Lottery, and actually probably wasn't a lottery win at all, as even
    small lotteries were illegal until 1934, when J. was 17! Perhaps her father
    won the football pools, which Littlewoods began in 1922.

Jean Anderson poses with her dolls, South Shields, 1935.

sister bought her a similar Christmas present, things didn't go according to plan. 'I believed in Santa – I was just a little girl. But all my faith in Santa was dashed when I got up and seen that doll hanging up with my little cousin's clothes on it, while my little cousin had no clothes on. They had been borrowed for the doll. I knew then that Santa hadn't brought it.' The baby probably wasn't too pleased either!

Other dolls were much less sophisticated. Mrs E.S. 'had a wooden betty which my uncle had made out of wood, and the eyes were burnt in with a poker, the nose and mouth and teeth were burnt in with a poker then painted. It went through five of us, and then it went under the oven to heat it for Sunday's dinner.' Billie C., born in 1923 in Benwell, also had a home-made doll. 'My first little dolly was a clothes peg, with two black eyes painted on it, and a nose and little bonnet put on the head, and a dress put on, and there was a little bar for the arms. I used to treasure it.' She also had a very special – if far from politically correct! – toy. 'I had, like a little gollywog, and it was mechanical. When you put a penny in its hand, or a ha'penny, it used to lift the hand up and put it in its mouth. It was a proper money box you know, and I used to think "Well the money's gone in, but how am I going to get it out?"'

At Christmas, parents would often make great efforts to provide something special. Jean W. remembers one wartime Christmas, when 'mam got all these Walt Disney little models. I don't know where she got them; she probably gave someone some eggs for them. And she got some old net curtains and made stockings, a beautiful stocking for Valerie, and put all these things in. And to give her this, was just so fantastic.'

Boys and their Toys

Little boys, on the other hand, were often given wooden or wind-up vehicles. Harry W. got a pedal car for Christmas. 'It was the pride of my life that pedal car, get in there, I used to think it was marvellous, it had these dials on, they were only painted dials but I thought that was marvellous.' In the early 1920s, Mary's brother got 'a little wind-up engine, with a tender with imitation coal on. We all crowded round him full of delight, because he'd got a present. And he loved that little engine.' Mr P.J., born in 1918, had 'a Hornby train, clockwork of course, and Meccano, and toy soldiers in a fort.' His contemporary, John T., got a surprising present at a Methodist Christmas party. 'It was a dray wagon with a couple of barrels on. I thought it was lovely. I spent hours playing with that, rolling the barrels off and on. Well, all these Temperance people giving a young boy a dray wagon with barrels of beer on!'

Without access to shop-bought fun, boys could be ingenious in devising toys. Tom H. of Hetton-le-Hole loved kite flying. He says, 'We never bought our kites in the shops, we made our own. If you could cadge half a roll of wallpaper off your mam, you would go to the grocers and get the hoops off the butter barrels. You cut one of them in half. You would make a kite shape with an ordinary cross piece with a half hub of the butter barrel round the top, and paste a piece of wallpaper on that. Adjust your strings to suit according to the balance of the kite, put your tailings on, usually rolled up bits of paper, or your mam would sometimes give you an old duster or something. We didn't know about aerodynamics in those days, but we knew what would make a kite fly.'

Two boys play with a toy car.

On a smaller scale, Ernie K. remembers making paper aeroplanes: 'A proper aeroplane with a tail on it, it used to fly and land.' Collinson B., growing up in wartime High Heaton, made more vicious aeroplanes. 'If you could get hold of some pen nibs, that was great, you used to break off the tips to leave two fangs sticking out. You would split the other end so you could put a paper flight on them, and make darts with them and fling them – those were lethal!'

Collinson had another hair-raising activity – making and firing 'clay boilers' in wartime bomb sites. A clay boiler was 'a rectangular thing with holes in the top and the end. You'd fire it to harden it, and stuff it with a petrol-soaked rag and set light to the rag. It would flame through the funnel and pour forth smoke, and we would run around to get the thing going, and leave a great smoke screen behind us.' Perhaps unsurprisingly he also made guns, combining firewood, hairpins, matches, and rubber bands (from lemonade bottle tops) into exciting contraptions. He wasn't the only one – Horsley H. made 'potato guns, which were little tubes and you pressed them into a potato and it took a piece out, you used to blow it out the end. And you had pea shooters, and high flyers, which were like a twisted piece of wire with a little propeller on and a little pin, when you pushed it up hard the little propeller flew off the top.'

In pre-war Sunderland, Jim G. and his friends were also making things. 'You could walk on tin cans with strings attached in your hands. But the biggest and best thing was, we used to have competitions, walking on stilts, which were made of scrap wood.' Jim also made his own spinning toy, using string and a cardboard milk bottle top. So many of his friends wanted one that 'it was not unknown for us to find our way into the dairy during the weekend, and help ourselves to a box of milk bottle tops!'

Even vehicles were worth a shot. Alan L., born in 1913, recalls that in Tynemouth, lads 'would get an old pram and they would take the pram wheels off and rig an axle up, and put a few planks of wood across, and they would have this sort of bogie thing.' His contemporary, John H., also remembers these 'bogies'. 'We used to get empty margarine boxes, and somehow or other we used to get four wheels, two pairs of wheels on an axle, which you fixed to the bottom of the margarine box, tie a piece of rope to the front and tow each other round in the margarine box.'

Sledges could be made in a similar way. Alan L. would join his friends sledging down Long Sands bank, Tynemouth, in the 1920s, in any sledge they could put together. 'A lad would knock up an apple box or something, with a little bit of steel binding tape, and make the best of it. Whereas if you had a pukka sledge you were really going places.'

A Wallsend girl plays on a sledge (*c.* 1945).

Or you could get adult help. After all, many fathers were working in industries where it was easy to work a bit of metal in your lunch break, and it hadn't been so very long since they were boys themselves. John H. says, 'The men were joiners and that sort of thing, and they could make sledges. And there was always men who worked in the engineering factories, who would get a length of steel strip to put on the bottom, to make the slides, you see.'

Men often made 'guards' or 'boolers' for their children, metal hoops propelled along with a hooked stick. Richard C. got one from his father during the First World War. 'I took my father's dinner over to the North Eastern Marina and when I went in he said, "I've got a guard for you" and that was it, I just wheeled it out.' Spinning tops also emerged from engineering shops and pit buildings. Tom H.'s grandfather worked in the pit. 'He would just go to the joiner's shop and say, "Have you got any spare bits of wood?" He would either carve it himself, or get the colliery joiner to do one in his spare time. I've seen me drive a top all the way to school, that's over a mile. You used to cover the top in brightly coloured chalks, and make it a kaleidoscope of colours when you're whipping it. Or you could jump it. I've seen lads who could make a top jump fifty or sixty yards. Sometimes go through somebody's window as well!'

Children from Thornley Infants' School play with toys.

Rough and Tumble

Not that you needed fancy equipment to have a laugh. Geordie children had a near infinite variety of ways to pass time in the quiet back lanes, with the help of some friends, and maybe a wooden stick or ball. Often these games had a distinct season. As John H., born in Gateshead in 1911, puts it: 'Suddenly it would be marbles, and then another time it would be

Two young boys, Fred and Foster, play cricket in a South Shields back lane.

cherry stone time, or as we called them cherry bugs, and another time it would be baseball time, or relievo. And who decided when we'd change from one sport to another? I don't know but it happened.'[9]

In 1920s Byker, according to Horsley H., 'You played leapfrog, you played hide and seek, and you played a game called kick the block. You used to put a tin on top of the grate, and everybody would get away. The one that was left would have to try and catch them and while he was away, if they kicked the block away he had to put it back, before he could catch anybody else. That used to last for ages.' He also played mounty kitty – one team of boys bending over in a long line (the last braced against a wall) and the other lot all leaping on their backs. Joe G. adds 'that was quite a rough game, because they would deliberately jump up in the air and land heavily so that the "horse" collapsed.'

As you might expect, the lads also played football in the back lanes. Alan L. of Tynemouth remembers: 'Footballs were too expensive to buy, so we would go to the local butcher. In those days they slaughtered their own beasts behind the shop. And we'd get a beast's bladder, and blow the bladder up and take it on the beach and play with it.' In the 1930s, the alleys near Joe G. were cobbled 'and it was a great event when they came round and concreted those back lanes and made them smooth, because you could play football there.'

Mr A. was also able to take advantage of a newly tarmacked street, 'which gifted us with three football pitches, the bottom pitch, the middle pitch and the big pitch. The bottom pitch was the hardest to play, because lorries and horses, carts carrying goods into Scots Yard, very often intervened in these enthusiastic games.' The middle pitch was difficult because it was between the high railings of the church hall, and a confectioner for the Co-op who worked the nightshift. The big pitch was best – but there, you had to grab a game when you could before the adults came along.'

By Peter J.'s time (the 1960s) the balls were quite different, made of 'very soft plastic, and it wasn't like hard balls like what it is today.

---

9   Relievo is a version of team hide and seek, with one team seeking and
    the other hiding (and trying to save their already captured team mates).
    Cherry stones here probably means throwing and catching them like jacks.

Two young lads play football.

They were just cheap and chatty I suppose, for two and six in old money, that's what we could afford.' Cheap balls had their downsides though. 'Three pots in, the back door was your goal in the back lane. Sometimes it would hit the glass which would burst your ball and then you would have to go back and get a new ball.'

Games for Girls

While the boys were getting their knees muddy and scraped, the girls were often in the house doing chores. According to Jim G., 'You never seen any girls in them days. They were all in the house, parents kept them in.' When girls did get out, they had different games to play, often involving 'boody'. As Nan L. of Newcastle explains, 'We used to play shops with all sorts of bits of boody, which was bits of broken china, glass, anything you could find.' Betty S. adds, 'You'd go around your family and ask them if they'd got any broken plates or saucers. We'd play, we used to call them boody shops – we used to chop the china up, and they were supposed to be sweets and things.'

Girls were also more likely to sing. Betty S. also 'used to play concerts in the backyard. We used to borrow our mother's lace curtains and

Girls play a game of shops, on Sandgate, Newcastle (*c.* 1898). (Lantern slide by Edgar
G. Lee, courtesy of Newcastle Libraries Local Studies collection)

dress up in them. And mother used to make things for you to play with,
like headdresses for to play concerts with.' And Frank F. remembers
'many singing games, usually played by girls as they were beneath the
dignity of the boys and nobody would be seen playing them!'

Skipping was a popular girl's game, although often with lads' help in
turning the ropes. Richard C. played in the streets of Wallsend in the
1910s. 'If you managed to pinch a length of your mother's clothes line,
you could get a couple of strong lads on each end of the rope and start
swinging it round and get, if you were lucky, eight girls in the middle
and really make it belt. Mind the lads who were swinging the rope gave
up before the girls, they could skip all day.'

Then there was 'itchy dabber', or 'bays', based on a chalk grid similar to
hopscotch. Tom H. says, 'Normally the dabber was an empty shoe polish
tin filled with sand or earth or something like that. You chucked your
dabber on the first square and hopped. You sort of hopped and kicked
ahead of you all the way. Mostly it was a girl's game but sometimes you
were swindled into taking part.' For Billie C., apple bobbing was fun for all

Children play on the Newcastle Quayside, 1890s. One has a skipping rope.

the family. 'The fruit man used to come up on a Sunday. We used to buy
fruit from him and we used to play ducky apple, cut the apples up and put
them in the water in a big bowl, and then put your head in, you know.'

Boys and girls both played marbles. Between the wars, marbles was
very popular, and there were plenty of connoisseurs. Tom H. says, 'Some
marbles were highly valued, a glass alley was your prized possession.
A marble was an ordinary plain thing, it was either made of clay, baked,
or they were made of glass and plain, but your glass alley was made
of lovely spiral colours.' Ernie K. 'used to play marbles in the gutter on
the way home. There were clay marbles, there was a "potty". If you
had an iron tonker, that was a big one, a steel one, that was worth
about thirty or twenty marbles.' As Joe G. explains, you could even spot
the regulars. 'You finished up with holes at the back of your thumb,
from flicking – you could always tell who were the good players, they
actually had holes in their thumbs and they had to stick a bit of plaster
over to go on playing.'

Mischief and Fighting

Kids could expect a clip round the ear if they misbehaved, but of course that often didn't stop them. The most popular trick was 'knocky nine doors'. Nan L. 'used to get a black thread, and we used to tie it on maybe Mrs Pearson's door, and we used to go about six doors along and tie it on her door.' Then they would knock on the doors, and wait. Done cleverly, as Richard C. recalls, 'you would see them playing war to get the doors open.' Better yet, Tom H. could arrange a bobbin, dowel, lolly stick and elastic band so that it would wind up. 'If you placed that on the window sill, as it unwound the lolly stick used to knock on the window, tap, tap, tap. And somebody would come out and say, "Who's tapping?" and nobody was there. You were round in the next street.'

In the 1910s, Mr O. of Jesmond and his mates 'used to go round the back lanes and smash the odd lamp and things. But of course we knew perfectly well if we were caught first the police would give us a good hiding, then your father would give you a good hiding as well, and you

A group of children stand in the street, in Brandling Village, Jesmond, taken *c.*1911. (Courtesy of Newcastle Libraries Local Studies collection)

took that risk.' Living near to engineering works, mines and shipyards gave ample opportunity for mischief. In the 1920s, Thomas G. lived in Gateshead beside the railway. 'There was fog signals, about the size of a ginger snap biscuit. Guards used to put them on the line, and when the trains used to go over them they used to send out a bang if there was a fog or any disruption, you see. We used to raid them, and throw bricks at them to make a sound.'

Then there were the scraps. As Richard C. puts it, 'If you had a battle with one of your mates, well, you had a battle and your mates stood round. But if you used your feet your mates disowned you. You'd have a battle and the next day it was forgot and you were pals again.' There were all sorts of reasons for a fight. John and Nan L. remember the gangs that formed around election time. Nan says, 'We used to have the time of our life with elections, you know. We used to walk round the street, you know, singing "vote vote vote for Mr Somebody". Whoever your parents voted for.' When they met a group supporting a rival politician, things got messy. John adds, 'There was a riot and another crowd coming the other way, you used to bash each other with these paper balls. It was a paper ball, tied up with string to make it like a hard ball – nobody got hurt.'

Other fights were more vicious and more territorial. Collinson B. and his friends from the choir regularly found their Friday night tram home from the centre of Newcastle disturbed by rivals. 'We competed with this family of kids, who were real urchins, real tough nuts from Abyssinia, for the front end of the tram. There were four of them and four of us, and we literally fought, brawled, much to the consternation of the passengers we fought and fought and fought. Unfortunately we gradually got outnumbered as we got to our stop and got off. I was always second-to-last off by which time Dicky Barker and I were getting a thorough pasting usually.'[10]

---

10 Abyssinia was a nickname for a council estate beyond Four Lane Ends.

Four

Out and About

The Tyneside streets have only quite recently become choked up with cars. In the 1930s, Billie C. remembers: 'When it was summer evenings, the mothers would come out and bring a cracket out and sit on it, sit and knit, and they used to talk and the kids were playing in the street and we could play out till nine o'clock.' Horse-drawn vehicles were a common – and popular – sight until at least the 1950s. Milk was sometimes brought round on a cart and ladled out into a basin, and Mr P.J. of Jesmond fondly remembers that 'sometimes the milkman would let my sister and me ride up the street in his trap.' On the streets of 1920s South Shields, Ernie K. says, 'In the hot weather, there used to be a cart, it used to have a sprinkler on the back to keep the dust down in the hot weather. All the lads would get their bare feet and follow the water cart, get the cold water on your feet.'

Trams became a feature of many Newcastle streets from around 1900. Mr R. was only 4 when the trams came to Cotesworth Road, Newcastle, in 1901, and remembers 'stepping over the tramlines – because I'd heard the bigger ones say the electricity would kill you.' Collinson B. provides a vivid description of the trams and buses of wartime Newcastle. 'We liked going in the open end, particularly at the

A Birtley District Co-operative Society horse-drawn delivery van waits outside Washington Co-op. (Ward Philipson Collection)

Gloucester Street, Elswick, 1913. Children are sledging in the background, and a flock of sheep crosses the road. (Courtesy of Newcastle Libraries Local Studies collection)

front, hanging over the railings and waving to passers-by. I dare say people used to fall out. The trams were always packed. The lights all had their wartime cowls on, and everybody smoked, so they were full of smoke and very dim. You couldn't see, literally, from one end of the tram to the other, upstairs.'

And all sort of things travelled by road, like the cattle brought into the heart of Newcastle. Mary lived near the Redheugh Bridge as a child, and her father warned her to stay away from the animals. '[The drovers] used to hit the poor animals with the stick, 'cause they were frightened and if they could run away, they would. And now and then one did get away, and they used to run in fear round the town. We were frightened of them, used to be terrified when we used to see the cattle coming.'

Street Sellers and Entertainers

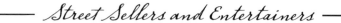

The streets were busy places, with a lot more people working and socialising out of doors, and the kids watched it all – especially if it involved food. Mary Bl. says, 'I always remember the muffin man coming round with the lovely basket and the white cloth and gorgeous muffins and crumpets, and he used to carry it always on his head.' Ice cream was, of course, a special favourite. Mr P.J. remembers the ice cream sold by 1930s firm Eldorado. 'It was sold in twopenny and fourpenny blocks, ready wrapped, and stored in chests on wheels which the driver, sitting behind, pedalled along.' Nancy Y., of the previous generation of Newcastle children, was not allowed any ice cream because, as her parents told her, the seller 'lived in the slums and he put his ice-cream barrel under his bed through the night!'

Almost anything that could be carried could be sold on the street. Mr F., born in Newcastle in 1909, remembers that when he was a child 'Jews used to come round with glass on their back, window frames. There used to be coopers coming round, they used to put rings on the poss tubs. On a Friday the gypsies used to come round selling buttons and thread, pictures and oil cloths. They would sit on the roadsides and smoke little clay pipes.'

Nancy Y. recalls that in turn-of-the-century Arthur's Hill 'there used to be women come down the back lanes with a barrow made of a box and two wooden handles. They used to have rubbing stone that they got from the quarry at the bottom of the street, and pipe clay, either blue or white.[11] They used to have sticks in the barrow, and sometimes they would have a poor little baby of their own, on top of all that rubbish. Another cry was a man that came round with a properly made barrow with a tank on full of lamp oil. Before the gas lighting appeared, everybody had to have a paraffin lamp. And the next man that came up was Richie, the fruiterer. He had one leg, and a lot of soft bananas on his barrow – "bananas, two a penny bananas".'

But perhaps the most colourful figure was the fishwife. In the 1910s, Mrs A. lived on Almond Street, Shieldfield, where 'the old fish woman, we called her Fanny Olley. She was a little fat body. She used to sway from side to side, and the basket on the top of her head would sway from side to side. She would shout her fish as she came down the street. We got a nice lump of fish from her, bake it in the oven, and partially stuff it, and parsley sauce. She wore a linen skirt, pleats and tucks round the bottom, an apron, a towel on her head rolled around and the basket on top of that.' Mary Bl. didn't so much remember the fishwife as the fish themselves, saying, 'The fishwife used to come up from Cullercoats, and her lovely petticoats, great full skirts, and the fish were practically alive, I may say. We once got a haddock, and I remember it was moving, and I dashed upstairs and put it in the bath, I couldn't bear it not to be in water. My mother said, "Well you'd better do it properly and add some salt!"' The haddock, of course, died.

Of course, it was in the sellers' interests to attract attention, whether working door to door or at a market. Markets in particular could be places full of wonder. According to Mr A., on one Sunday morning on the 1920s Quayside, an inquisitive child might spot an escape artist, racing tipsters, games of darts, and sellers of fruit, ice cream, and chocolate 'so hard you had to break it with a hammer but it kept you quiet on a Sunday afternoon'. Another attraction was Mr Gallon,

---

11 Rubbing stone would be used to smooth any rough edges on hearths and
    doorsteps, while pipe clay is a fine clay which cleaned and whitened them.

A Cleadon village fishwife poses with her baskets.

sarsaparilla salesman, with 'pith helmet, Malacca cane, a pair of jodhpurs, would have been more at home on a sixteen-stone cavalry major, but he sold that sarsaparilla because he had to make a living.'[12]

Others were simply selling entertainment. As a small child in about 1900, Nancy Y. was at home ill 'when a dirty old man with a dirty old bear came down the street. The bear used to dance in front of the window to entertain me, and the poor old man got a penny. Then I fell on the floor with whooping cough.'

Mr C.R. remembers that in Edwardian times 'the Bigg Market on a Saturday night was full of turns, strong men snapping chains on their chest. It was lit up with paraffin flares then. And there was a blind concertina player, he was famous, he used to play on request. And a chap, he had a leather cup on his head, and he would get a cricket ball, throw the ball up and catch it.'

Swalwell Hoppings.

---

12 Malacca is a kind of rattan often used for walking canes in India.

Once a year, the ultimate combination of exotic entertainment and slick salesmanship was to be enjoyed, at least partly for free, at fairs often known as Hoppings. Smaller events of this name were held in Edwardian Swallwell and Ryton, among other places, but the star attraction was the Town Moor Hoppings, held every Race Week. In the 1920s, Mary trekked out to the Town Moor every year. 'The steam engines used to make a lot of water, and it was always clarty. And poor Walter, his feet got stuck in the clarts and he lost his sandshoes. And you hadn't any money to spend on the sideshows, but there would be the dancing girls, and the barkers, shouting out what was on. The Wild West shows, the cowboys used to be at the front – and at the boxing booths, the boxers used to be outside putting on a bit show. In fact people often used to say there was more going on outside than there was inside. And of course there was the steam organs, the coconut shies, the horses, that go up and down and round and round, and the mats and the cakewalk.' The Hoppings even had a cinema screen, some years before the first cinemas opened in the region in 1909.

Out on the Town

In the early days, films were played on white sheets put up in church halls, theatres or even across the street. In Rowlands Gill in 1910, as Joseph F. remembers, the Cameron brothers had bought a cinematograph. 'They had a big hut in the garden. They had this white sheet and put it at the front, and they made little seats. And you took pins to get in. They showed you a good show, it was something worth a see.'

Within a few years there were proper cinemas, charging real money. Miss J.S., born in 1917, says, 'My birthday is in November and my parents used to give me some money to take friends to the cinema. That was my birthday treat. Jackie Coogan films were the ones, at the time.' Hannah W. of Denton was two years older and rather less honest. 'It was a penny to get in. If there was six or seven of us, perhaps only two of us would gan in, and we would open the door and let the other five in through the side door when the manager Mr Scott wasn't looking. I can remember one night Mr Scott said to my dad, "I've got a really full house but the takings is down!"'

A young boy poses in the uniform of the Hippodrome Cinema, 1926.

Then there was the theatre. In around 1885, Mrs B.C. was surprised to find herself in trouble for repeating a song. A young woman came on stage and sang a song which asked, 'Why can't dear little girls do just the same as the men?' and suggested women should be able to propose to men. Her mother told her in no uncertain terms she was not to sing the song; it was not fit for children! Joe G., too, got in trouble for repeating what he heard at the pantomime – in this case 'oompa, oompa, stick it up your jumper.' 'We had a little boy with us at the theatre, and we took him home. We did that for his parents and they were – that was filth! They said we were teaching their son filth. And I thought what's wrong with stick it up your jumper, and I didn't know, you see ...'

This certainly didn't put Joe G. off visiting Newcastle's 1930s theatres. 'One year we all queued up and got into the gods. There mustn't have been enough people down in the pit, and we were all led downstairs. The seats weren't wooden, they were plush seats, and I sat and watched the pantomime. I was king!' Not everyone had such fun. Mamie, a generation earlier, recalls the year that 'I and two other children were allowed to sit in a box. We felt that was very important, but we were right on top of the orchestra, which was too loud, and the principals address themselves to the main part of the house. We felt left out, and the make up on the faces of the cast and chorus was almost grotesque. I remember thinking it wasn't so marvellous to be the kind of person able to pay for a box!'

Or you could go to watch a football match. Bella P. remembers that in about 1920 'the Leazes Park was fantastic, and it was only sixpence to get in the Gallowgate end and sixpence at the Leazes end, at the football matches. They used to open the gates for the last ten minutes and we all used to get in there for nowt.' The Edwardian era was a golden age for Newcastle United, and Ethel A.'s father was in the thick of it. 'I would be about six, and I remember you see, at half time you could get in free. I seen my father on the field and the ball hit him – he had his own lovely teeth and it hit him in the mouth. And the blood! Of course there was missing teeth ... I went home and I says I'm never going to watch football again, they're killing me father!'

Parks and Wasteland

The progression of St James' Park from park to football stadium was well under way at this point, with the ground fenced in and stands on all sides. But there were still plenty of parks – many Victorian in origin – for children to play in. Nun's Moor Park in the early 1900s was a mix of the unfamiliar – a deer park – and the very recognisable, as Mrs B. remembers: 'We took my brother, when we were told not to take him, to the swing park in Nuns Moor Park. We put him on the swings, and he fell off and got gravel in his knees and his face. We had to take him back to my grandmother's to get him cleaned up before we ever thought of going back home!'

Children play in a Newcastle park. (Ward Philipson collection)

For an active child, such parks could be a second home. Hannah W. of Denton says, 'You could climb out of the window onto a tree and into the Dene, they were so near! You could play up the park, your parents would perhaps just open the door and shout your name, "Your dinner's ready!"' Similarly, Betty S. 'used to go to the Heaton Park, and she used to give wor some jam and bread and a bottle of concentrated orange, used to put it in a bottle, and away we went, we were away all day, nobody bothered, nobody said anything and we used to come home when we were hungry.'

But many children also made playgrounds of the disused or forgotten corners of town. Mrs E.C. haunted some wasteland in the 1900s. 'It got the name of the Bog, but it was rather a bonny place, grass and flowers and a lot of bricks. I think Lemington glassworks must have been near at hand. There was a lot of glass around – not glass you could cut yourself on, more like tubes. And we used to build houses with the bricks.' Forty years on, Collinson B. played in the disused building sites and ruined buildings of war-torn Newcastle. His favourite spot was amongst the remnants of Red Hall, where the prisms of old chandeliers could still be unearthed from the rubble.[13]

Some places were even less safe. John L., whose mother often left him to his own devices, found a surprising, if dangerous, playground under Newcastle's streets. 'You could walk from the Quayside right up just past St Thomas' Church, in Haymarket, underground, you could do that. Well, it was very black. You had to take matches all the time, great long matches, you see. We got caught a few times – the policeman used to hit you with his cape. He'd hit you with his cape and it would knock you for six.'[14] More responsible parents might at least attempt to make some

---

13 Red Hall was another name for Benton Park (also known as Benton
    Park Hall, or Benton House – but not Benton Hall, which was next door!)
    This late-eighteenth-century house was demolished in the 1930s
    to make way for housing, but this in turn was stalled by the war.
    The street to the front of Benton Park is still called Red Hall Drive.

14 It's likely that John's explorations were in the Victoria Tunnel, a brick waggonway
    tunnel built between Spital Tongues and the Ouseburn in 1842, which does
    indeed pass near St Thomas' church – though by his day, around 1900, this did
    not reach all the way to the river – so perhaps he knew other, now lost, routes.

areas out of bounds, as when Elsie B.'s father banned her from Clive Street in North Shields. Clive Street was down on the dockside, busily frequented by itinerant sailors and prostitutes: 'Terrible the people living in there, they'd frighten you.'

Fields and Woods

Until quite recently, even in the heart of Newcastle you were never that far away from a farmer's field. In the 1900s, Nancy Y. would nip across the back lane to Mr Brewis, who kept two cows on Town Moor, Newcastle, and housed them in the New Mills windmill! 'The milk was fresh and nice and creamy, better than any of the milk you get now. Then after the cows had calved, there was some special milk, the first milk from the cow. My mother had a recipe for making a beautiful custard pudding with that special milk.' Just around the corner you could also buy butter and eggs direct from a farmer.

Not that money always changed hands. Near Richard C.'s Wallsend home, around 1920, 'there was apple trees and pear trees all round. I used to pinch apples from there. And it was lovely just to go into the turnip field and pull a one. And mind they were big turnips.

Children play in the paddling pool, Jarrow Park, 1937.
(Courtesy of Newcastle Libraries Local Studies collection)

About the size of a football sometimes.' A few years later in South Shields, Ernie K. was also trying his luck: 'We used to pinch tateys and turnips from the farmers' fields. We'd light a fire, and put the potatoes in the fire – they were burnt to bits on the outside, and inside was hard as a house!'

Every quiet spot could be the inspiration for fun and games. Peg H. lived near a railway embankment, near Paradise, in the 1930s. 'The branches of these two trees, the way they were crossed made like a seat, and we used to sit in there and pretend we were sitting in an aeroplane.' Mary Bl. remembers the edge of the West End in the 1910s: 'beyond that was all grass and trees and even a pond. I can remember going home dripping several times, I'd probably had been thrown in!'

And of course some corners of Tyneside were truly in the countryside, so you could get out into the wild relatively easily, whether by walking or other means. J.L. got a bike in 1902: 'I'd be about ten. I jumped on the bicycle on Bath Lane and I had to turn up Bath Terrace, I couldn't turn up there and I went up into the wall with the bicycle.'

Horsley H. went on long hikes with friends, sometimes aided by the very cheap public transport. 'For a ha'penny you could get a tram from the top of Heaton Road used to take you to Throckley. Or to Scotswood Bridge. So we used to get the ha'penny tram to there and walk to Winlaton mill and go blackberrying you know.' Joseph F. had the woods of Rowland's Gill on his doorstep: 'We were never away from the river, in the summertime. Mother would give us a bottle of ginger beer, stottie cake, sandwich or something, and then we gan away for the day and come back at night after the sun had gone down. Where we lived there was a meadow, full of flowers. We used to all get in there and sit making daisy chains. And of course there used to be little fish in the river, minnows. We used to make a little pool away from the river, and when we had catched them we used to put them in the pool, and then set them away again.'

Generations of small boys revelled in seeking out conkers, blackberries, and birds' eggs. Horsley H. remembers that in the 1920s 'you never got wrong for bird nesting, so you used to go out looking for thrushes' eggs, and blackbirds' eggs.' Children like Collinson B. roamed

Alfred 'Kipper' Herring, the fourth child of a Gateshead cycle builder, shows off one of his father's wares (c. 1915).

for miles in the countryside, 'eating liquorice root, eating cinnamons or smoking them, and eating carlins.[15] We used to dig up potatoes and use them as ammunition, walking all the way along the Derwent to the old coke works at Derwenthaugh, singing all the way back. We'd go to the balloon barrage, down to the Coast Road, even to Little Benton farm, to the old slag heaps down there, occasionally stumbling across bunches of men playing something illegal. They always used to chase us.'[16]

Sunday schools also organised trips to the countryside, often with competitions. Dennis B. went from Newcastle 'to Ponteland usually, a farm there. There were prizes for races, egg and spoon races, and that

---

15 Carlin peas were a particular favourite of Geordie children, especially on the Sunday before Palm Sunday, when they were often handed out for free. There is a traditional rhyme in the area – 'Tid, Mid, Miseray, Carlin, Palm, Pace-Egg Day' – which helps with remembering the order of events during Lent.

16 These men would have been playing pitch and toss, a coin-tossing gambling game, which really was illegal at the time.

general sort of thing. I won one once, a little aeroplane that went round on a string.' For Mrs E.A. of South Shields, the food was the important bit. 'There were some people called Pearson who went to the Chapel, and they had a wholesale business, sweets and they used to have a stall in the field. We used to all sit down on the ground and we all got a bag of cakes. Then of course we used to come home quite content.'

From 1907, Scouting (and three years later, Guiding) encouraged city kids to get out into the fresh air of the countryside. Before the First World War, Joseph F. often camped with the Scouts in Winlaton woods. He remembers: 'We used to light the fire and put the carrier on, fill it with water and boil it and make the tea. We had a stove where you could cook everything.' Jim B. loved making the annual trip from Birtley to Bowes for a camp with midnight orienteering thrown in. 'The scout master would take us out on the moors, take every compass off us, and say, "Right, find your way back to the camp."'

There was also a militaristic element. J.F. remembers 'the church hall where you used to gan in and do a bit drilling and that, you know. What Scouts do. That was a nice thing to have for a laddy.' Girls' experience,

Children play in a farm barn on a Sunday school outing from St James' Congregational Church (later URC), Newcastle, 1931.

Boy Scouts and their leaders, Sandyford, Newcastle (*c.* 1910).

of course, was more genteel – though it still freed them to learn skills like knot-tying which were more usually thought of as boys' activities. For Miss J.S., Guiding was the highlight of the week. 'I think Guiding really saved school days for me, because I enjoyed it and I was doing practical things. I did quite well at Guides, went on and did all sorts of badges.' She particularly enjoyed camping, which was sometimes 'very very wet. We went to Raby Castle and Lady Baden-Powell came. I remember we had to provide cucumber sandwiches for her tea, and providing cucumber sandwiches at camp was quite interesting! And I remember hating washing up the porridge.'[17]

17 J.S. may be thinking of the Scout's Jamboree of 1936, which was attended by
   Lord and Lady Baden-Powell. However, she would have been 18 by this point,
   so perhaps this was an earlier visit to the area by the Guiding Movement's founder.

An alternative to Scouting, in some areas, was the Pathfinders, set up in connection with the Co-operative movement. Eileen McKinnon was 11 when, in 1945, her mother took her to the Benwell Pathfinders. 'It was mainly social activities but we did get our little Pathfinder card to join and we paid a penny, I think, a week and we had to sit down and learn your Pathfinder Pledge. But it was always group games, co-operative games where we all had to work together and it was boys and girls, and they taught us a little bit history about the Co-operative Movement.'

The Beach

The beach was a massive draw for kids like Horsley H. of Byker, even if time was short when you got there. After a long walk 'you had to paddle in the water to say you'd been in the sea, then you walked back home again.' In the 1920s, Frank G. and his friends made a game out of it: 'We used to go down regularly to the beach, which would probably be about three miles away, and our parents used to give us a ha'penny to go on the tram. We used to race the tram – if it was very busy, we could beat it down to Roker. We'd use the ha'penny to buy sweets or something like that!'

For the 1923 Consett Poor Children's Trip, a charabanc belonging to Atkinson and Browell of Consett, takes children to Spanish City, Whitley Bay.

Children from further afield would just have to wait for their chapel or Sunday school annual trip to the sea – like Joseph F. they would 'see the sea once a year'. Dorothy S. would walk down with her Sunday school to get the train to Whitley Bay from Heaton, singing 'Jesus loves me, this I know'. Around 1920, Annie G. of Blanchland sometimes travelled for

At Cullercoats, children play on the rocks and with a half-submerged set of cart wheels. (Courtesy of Newcastle Libraries Local Studies collection)

three hours in a hay cart to get to Whitley Bay. Each summer, thousands of children from Northumberland and County Durham clambered on to 'brakes' – horse-drawn or open-top buses – for the journey to Whitley Bay, South Shields, Roker, or another inviting beach. To get to South Shields from Edwardian Birtley, Reece E. 'used to set away at half six in the morning, and stayed til we could get the men out the pubs, at six or seven at night.' These were being replaced by charabancs, motorised open-top vehicles, with 'long seats, and an alleyway up one side and there was an adult sat at each end and the children in the middle so that we didn't tumble out' recalls Annie G.

Most children would arrive at the beach clutching a bag of food, often pie and buns. Their pennies would go on ice cream and, more surprisingly, on tea, which was sold by the teapot, with a deposit for the return of the empty pot. In Whitley Bay before the First World War, Mamie remembers that you could splash out at Fry's Boathouse. 'It was an upturned boat turned into a café, or a café constructed to look like a boat. They sold the most delightful singing hinnies, full of lard and dripping with butter and stuffed with currants.'[18] And at a pinch you could always catch your own, like Miss J.S. and her family, who went to Ryhope beach with nets

---

18 A singing hinny is a North Eastern form of griddle cake, made with
    flour, salt, lard, butter, baking powder, milk, and currants, sometimes
    with additional spices or alcohol. 'Singing' refers to the sizzling noise
    it makes when cooking, and 'hinny' is just a term of endearment –
    it comes from honey, although no honey is involved in a singing hinny!

Miss J.S. and her father shrimping on the beach at Ryhope.

Children enjoy donkey rides on Tynemouth beach (*c.* 1898). (Courtesy of Newcastle Libraries Local Studies collection)

'made with bamboo canes, and a wire D, and mother knitted the mesh out of very strong crochet cotton.' They returned home with pounds of shrimp to eat with buttered toast.

All the resorts tried to attract more day trippers. Edwardian Seaton had a troupe of pierrots, as Tom K. remembers: 'They came on the sands every year, we children used to love them. They used to put up a stage among the sand dunes and we used to give them our pennies at the end.' Mary M. recalls that South Shields at the same time had 'shuggy boats and marquees, and it was tuppence to have a dance to the band.' In the 1920s, when George P. visited Seaburn, 'there was tents, and these fellows building great big country scenes, castles and things like that with sand.'

Whitley Bay had a swimming pool carved into the rock, and increased its appeal with the opening of Spanish City in 1908. Margaret H. of Prudhoe visited in the 1920s, not long after the iconic dome had been added. She says, 'We never had the money to go on the roundabouts, but we used to watch. There were amusements inside as well, telling your fortune and things like that.'

Living near the sea, or staying with relatives, opened up a whole new range of possibilities for the enterprising child. Horsley H.'s uncle took him beachcombing at Seaton Sluice. 'There was quite a lot of money that people had lost, so we used to dash down and grab all these pennies. You had to clean it, but it was still money!' They would also play cricket, and 'duck stones' – throwing rocks at a cairn – on the rocky beach. According to Alan L., Tynemouth lads made the most of their opportunities 'fishing, going round the rocks and getting crabs. They had the chance of getting off in a boat, they learned to row, you could go in and readily swim.' On the other side of the Tyne, his contemporary Ernie K. was also enjoying life. 'At the northern end of Marsden beach there's a place called Camel's Island which is shut off at high tide. We used to take a clothes horse and blankets, we used to be camped there safe. You never slept or nowt like that, you just carried on.'

But whatever they did there, everyone would agree with Annie G. that 'it was a great thing to go to Whitley Bay'.

Five

Education

Early Days

Wherever and whenever they lived, from the age of 5 onwards, the school day was a common factor in the lives of all the children in this book. Education only become compulsory in 1880, so some of our informants' parents would never have gone to school. But they themselves worked their way from the nursery class through a series of 'standards'. How long they had to stay depended upon the date, as the school leaving age steadily climbed. It was 10 in 1880, 11 in 1893 and 12 six years later; then raised to 14 in 1918, and higher still after the Second World War. Some were glad to see the back of school, while others felt they had to leave, to help mother at home or begin earning a wage. Only a few could stay in education for longer, paying fees or winning a scholarship onto special courses like teacher training or engineering.

Nancy Y. started school at Todd's Nook School, Arthurs Hill, in 1903. 'I didn't like the look of the teacher so I put up with her for a week or two. It was in a big room, there was four classes in it, and I'd got my eye on a teacher across the road, so I went and put myself in that class. When my teacher shouted my name on the register I sent my voice over, "Yes teacher". After about four days she thought the voice wasn't coming from where it should, and she looked over and pulled me by the hair back to where I should belong.'

Boys line up in a school playground, possibly at Brighton Grove School,
Newcastle-upon-Tyne.

Horsley H. soon settled in to his school in Byker, 1920. 'You got carried
away with playing with little toys and things like this that they gave you.
Some kids, it used to be a terrible job to try and get them to stay there.
But I got used to it quite early.' A few years later, Billie C. started school
in the West End. 'I cried because my mam went away and I was left.
But then I had an older sister, two years older than me, and she was still
in the classes that were near the infants school. I knew, our Lotty's there,
if anything happens I can always run to her.'

Before 1891, all education had to be paid for, and for some time after
this, pupils were expected to contribute to the school's funds. Elizabeth
N.'s school in Gateshead charged a penny a week, 'and if you hadn't your
penny you used to have to stand on the seat. Everybody knew you hadn't
paid your fare.' This was a real problem for very poor children like her
contemporary John L. He says, 'I'd probably go for half a day because

you used to have to pay a penny, and pennies was bad to get hold of, you know. I went to a place, Docherty's School. I remember doing two or three days there, and I was always getting caned because I couldn't do the work. And the finish, this master got under my skin and I picked the ink-well up and I threw the ink-cup at him. I run away and I never went back to school again.'

Teachers and Classrooms

Into the twentieth century, almost anyone could teach, although female teachers were usually unmarried. Billie C.'s 'teachers had high leg boots on, and all with long skirts, and spectacles on the end of their nose. Some of them were very old, but none of them were ever married. Another of John L.'s abortive attempts at education featured 'the headmaster, nine times out of ten, he was coming in intoxicated. And he had a headmistress, was a woman about six foot, easy six foot, and she used to chew chalk. And when it come to the pay day for the staff, this master used to get up on the platform and say, "You can all go home" and that was the end of your schooling for that particular time.'

Newcastle Royal Grammar School boys snapped for the *Evening World* at the start of the summer holidays (*c.* 1930).

Still, a lack of formal training didn't always mean bad teaching. In Sunderland in 1924 Miss J.S. went to 'a little private school which had only about twelve pupils. There were three teachers, but they hadn't got certificates. And some education act came in, and the school had to close. And I learned more in the four terms that I was there than when I went to the high school.'

Many schools had large rooms with several classes (sometimes mixed sex and age), with or without partitions. Norah C. remembers Todd's Nook School having seats 'just like the football field ones, a lot of stairs, no individual desks or anything.' There was often a central fire, where dinners and tea flasks were kept warm on cold days. Mrs E.C. recalls that in the 1920s 'we had a great big fire on. I remember one girl, her parents had a fish and chip shop – and if that girl got near that big fire with her clothes, the smell of fish and chips would reek the place out!'

Larger schools were sometimes single sex, like Dame Allan's School, Newcastle, which had tight regulations on the subject. Mary Bl. explains: 'The girls were downstairs and the boys were upstairs, and we were not allowed to even look at them. We used the back door and they used the front door. My sister-in-law was caught walking along with a boy to school one day. She was given a long lecture that she was not allowed to meet the boys out of school, or in for that matter. When she could get a word in edgeways she said, "But it's my brother!"'

Of course, when you did allow the sexes to mix, things changed, as Ernie K. recalls: 'There was girls in the class as well! From being a runny nosed jersey kid, there's girls in the class, you're starting to wash your face at dinnertime you know, which you didn't do at the boys' school, and you put a tie on. At dinner time the girls lifted the desk lids up and put make up on, and came to school with earrings, and they had to take them out before they went to class – twenty lads and twenty lasses, you can imagine, that was great! You started to tidy yourself up, you didn't polish your shoes at 14, but 15 to 16 you started.'

Margaret M. was born blind. That meant she couldn't go to school near her family's home in Stamfordham, but instead was sent to board at the Newcastle Blind School. This was 'a very old-fashioned school. When you went in, they were standing there with a toilet roll and a cape to put around your shoulders, the enamel plate and a tooth comb, and they

Children at the Royal Victoria School for the Blind. (Courtesy of Newcastle Libraries Local Studies collection)

went through your hair while your parents watched, even though you'd had your hair done the night before. And then you went upstairs and had it washed again!' Here, expectations for the blind children were low and the dresses apparently so horrible that 'my mother used to change me in the taxi on the way home so nobody saw the uniform!'

Lessons

Young children learned to write using slates, then moved on to dip pens. In the 1920s, Mr P.J. 'used to write on slates with slate pencils, which squeaked horribly, or in exercise books with pens with steel nibs and ink from ink-wells filled with greyish ink.' Collinson B.'s impression of school during the Second World War was 'putting your head in the desk, which smelled of plasticine and milk and ink. Making ink, of course – the ink-wells, and the pens you were always dished out with, and the blots you could never avoid, blots all over the place.'

Lessons, of course, tended towards the formal, with rote learning and an emphasis on English and mathematics. Members of Mrs E.S. of Sunderland's history class couldn't go home until they got a question right. John H. remembers learning long speeches by rote, some of which stayed with him for a lifetime: 'For instance, Wolsey's speech on fallen greatness. And Portia's speech "The quality of mercy is not strained", and the Seven Ages of Man. I can repeat the thirty-two counties of Ireland! And I learned the whole of the "Ancient Mariner".'

And then there was homework. Joe G. won a scholarship, but was terrified when another boy told him what to expect. 'He said at Dame Allan's they get three hours homework a night, and I remember waking up in the night and thinking "I can't manage three hours homework a night!"' He was even more worried when they started school. '[The others] all had school blazers and things; I had nothing at that time. They all had brand new haversacks, and I had an old army kit bag. And I felt terribly inferior, walking to these people, because they were all, what I thought, posh kids. I found out later most of them were from homes very like mine, but possibly not so many kids in them, so they had a little bit more.'

A group of girls sit reading at Benwell Library (*c.* 1950). (Courtesy of Newcastle Libraries Local Studies collection)

While some schools merely drilled in the basics of the '3 Rs', others provided wider opportunities. From Heaton Technical School, Horsley H. got trips out to Jesmond Dene learning about wood, to the Laing Art Gallery and even to view the mummies on display at the Hancock Museum. As a young girl in the late 1920s, Billie C.'s class would sometimes walk together from Cannon Street School to the nearest library. Libraries were much more forbidding places then: 'The teacher used to say, "Now what do you do now?" And the children always used to stand up straight, shoulders back, and [raises finger to her mouth] do that with your fingers, because you were told, no sound at all, in the library. And of course the librarians were all elderly people, with their hair fastened straight back in a bun and glasses on the end of their nose. We used to go and sit on the little chairs that was there, and the teacher used to read out of a book, because we didn't have a lot of books up at the school because there wasn't the money.'

Boys and girls had different lessons to learn, especially in private schools. Mrs R.'s school, Causley House, Newcastle, was clearly only teaching girls from well-off families. The curriculum was 'mostly English, and arithmetic, and French – we had a French madame. We had a dancing mistress came from Darlington, she came every week. And we learned gardening; Miss Jones was very keen on the garden. And music lessons, too, singing, and dancing, like the polka, ballroom dancing, and country dancing as well, which we loved. And we had hockey, and lacrosse, we played in the grounds. And posture, posture, oh yes, we had gym every week.'

Similarly the singularly pointless knitting classes Rebecca B. experienced in Edwardian Gateshead were only forced on girls, if of a different class. She remembers: 'We used to get a great big ball of thick wool on a Wednesday afternoon knitting, and we used to have big long needles. And we used to knit a whole lump and then who'd knitted the most got some marks for it. And then when we'd finished, it was pulled out and wrapped up and then put on the needles. The same ball of wool.' Mrs E.C.'s convent school needlework classes were equally unappealing. 'A great big ugly garment next to your skin, made of calico, and rough, you know, no vest next to your skin just this chemise. We used to sew these, by the time the chemise were finished they used to be dirty. Kids handling them for weeks!'

Mrs E.A.'s classes in cookery, sewing and knitting were clearly designed to train the housewives of the future. Around 1920, Thelma W. had 'housewifery' classes. 'This teacher, we called her "hot soapy water". Everything, "use hot soapy water!"' Equally telling is what girls like M[ary] Brown (at Dame Allens, a highly respected school) did not study. 'We did a little biology, but very, very little, and no chemistry or anything in that line. The boys did it, but it wasn't thought that girls should do that kind of thing.'

Boys meanwhile had a more rugged experience. Born in 1905, Mr C. was 7 years old when he was sent to the Northern Counties Orphanage in Jesmond – which had its own school – after his father died. It was strict, but stood him in good stead for the future. 'We had a lovely gym downstairs and they had mats for boxing. If anybody had a grudge against any other lad, if there was a row, the teacher used to say, "Look, if you want to get it out your system come to me, I'll referee, then you can bang it out with each other."'

Boys and girls both got physical exercise, but inevitably of different types. Jim G. played 'football, cricket which I didn't like, boxing I did like: where the railway used to be in Deptford, they'd taken all the sleepers

Girls playing hockey at Gateshead Secondary School.

Gender separation: girls in a cookery class at Dean Road School, South Shields, 1912, and boys in the woodwork room of the Royal Grammar School, Newcastle.

up and levelled it off and we used that as a football and cricket ground. I used to get murder off my dad, when you used to fall down, you used to be cut — it used to take the skin off your hands, you know.' Meanwhile at Dame Allan's, Mary Bl. 'did what we called gym, which was more like drill really. We did later get ropes and climbing frames and a horse.' Drill is also remembered by Nancy L., who was born in 1900 and educated at Snow Street School, Newcastle. 'We had drill in the school yard, with dumbbells, and long poles, and club swinging and all that. A sergeant major from Fenham Barracks used to come and train us.'

Mrs E.C. went to a Catholic school in Newcastle: 'There was about three teachers and the rest was nuns. Sister Mary Michael, what a sweet lady she was, she used to read stories from out the book, and at play time she used to sell sweets, for a ha'penny we could get a bag of sweets. We did a lot of religion, too much religion. When you first went in the morning, you assembled and there was prayers and hymns, especially on a Friday morning there was a lot of hymns. We enjoyed singing the hymns. The angelus would ring for twelve o'clock. As soon as the angelus rung all the class would stand up and say their prayers.'

Special Occasions

Certain special days punctuated the school calendar. Horsley H. remembers: 'You had all the different days, St George's Day, and Empire Day, and you all got dressed up. If there were any kids in the Cubs, or Boys Brigade, or Brownies, anything like that, they came in with their uniform. For Empire day, they put the flag out. You sang one or two patriotic songs, and all the classes lined up, and then naturally you finished off with God save the King.'

Not everyone got so involved. Henry K.'s father had fought in the First World War, and died in 1925 when Henry was 8. His mother was left with a small army pension which she considered poor thanks for her husband's years of service, and so she gave Henry instructions for Empire Day. 'I would march past the flag but I hadn't to salute. Well naturally the master used to say "come out". But I think he was quite satisfied with my mother's explanation because he never said anything.'

Still, a royal visit or celebration was a very special day. When Mrs B.C. was 8, in 1885, the Prince of Wales visited Tyneside.[19] 'When we all got in our position on this hill, above Hebburn Quay, we formed the

19 This was Prince Albert Edward, later Edward VII
    (who gave his name to the Edwardian era).

Wallsend children salute as they march past the flag on Empire Day.

Prince of Wales' feather. And when the boat came in, and we all saw him waving his handkerchief, we all stood up and waved to him. When we were going home they started throwing the fireworks up. I was afraid of them so I started to cry.' Nancy L. was 10 in 1910 when George V was crowned, and recalls 'a very big event in the football ground. They had a display of exercises, dumbbells, club swinging. And all the boys from different schools had different coloured caps, red white and blue – and they formed the flag.'

Mischief and Punishment

In spite of the threat of the 'school board man' – who would, as Richard C. puts it, 'just hump you along' to school if he caught you playing truant – some remained unconvinced of the merits of schooling. Mr M.R., whose parents moved around Newcastle's West End a lot, decided that 'no school was going to keep me in. They had eight-foot iron rails round the playground, at the only school that kept me in.' Margaret R., who attended the Stephenson Memorial School in the 1930s, also admits, 'I played truant a few times. I used to have myself a walk down the old turnpike road whenever it was sewing lessons! I was always found out. Because you never had a watch in those days – and I used to think, it was such a long time, "I'll go home now." And it was the middle of the afternoon!'

Jack R. was able to take rebellion one stage further when he took part in a school strike, one of a national wave of strikes amongst urban schoolchildren over the summer of 1911. 'We were supposed to have a half day off for what's called Royal Oak Day, and they didn't give us it.[20] So we left school in the morning and just stopped off in the afternoon. And the next morning the headmaster had the strikers and the non-strikers, he said the non-strikers could go home but the strikers had to stop at school. Mr Bowen ordered us all into the hall and told us what he was going to do with the strikers – he was going to get

A class of boys from Wingrove Primary School, Fenham are caught in an unusually informal pose, *c.* 1924. (Courtesy of Newcastle Libraries Local Studies collection)

20 Royal Oak Day is 29 May. It celebrates the Restoration of the Monarchy
    in 1660, and is commonly associated with freedom from tyranny.

the cane out! We just went on the rampage, we just ran out through the doors!'

With some honourable exceptions – like Mrs R.'s teacher, who would merely 'tick us off terribly if we weren't polite' – corporal punishment was the norm. Joe G. says, 'We had a teacher at school when I was six, who had a big black ebony ruler. You put your knuckles on the desk and you did your tables, and if you didn't know your tables he hit you on those knuckles, with the ebony ruler. I knew my tables extremely well!'

Punctuality and cleanliness were highly prized, and latecomers were often caned. Rebecca B. remembers that at Prior Street School, Nuns Lane, 'if you forgot your handkerchief twice you had to go to the mistress' room. You got a strap or the cane. And if anybody hadn't polished their boots they got the strap or the cane.' In Edwardian Sunderland, Charles D.'s headmaster had a sliding scale of punishments with the cane. 'If you were late you used to get three straps. Then if your shoes weren't clean, or your hair wasn't clean, you used to get another one. And if we'd been playing three holes, marbles, and your hands were dirty you used to get slapped for doing that. And if they caught you spitting on your hands, and rubbing them to make them fetch the heat back again, you used to get another one.'

Some teachers were deeply resented for brutality, but others – like the master at Mr C.'s orphanage school, Newcastle – somehow kept their pupils' respect. 'I've seen the boss when I couldn't answer a simple thing, he'd lamp me across the face. And perhaps five or ten minutes after, he'd come out and play football with the lads, as if nothing had happened. When he came in, he was right as rain and you were right as rain.'

Some teachers clearly enjoyed the power they had over pupils. Richard C.'s Wallsend class were playing darts into the ceiling with their dip pens when a master came in. Seeing a pen in the ceiling, he made its owner sit underneath it. 'He said, "You'll soon know when it comes down."' On another occasion someone stole and hid the same teacher's cane. 'He said, "Well, you'll all get it when I do find it." He just used to mark our name down on the blackboard, how many smacks we were getting. When he did find it, we were all standing in a line there and he was just looking at the blackboard, ten for you, six for you, and he hammered us.'

— *Sunday School and Choir* —

Whether Catholic, Church of England or Nonconformist, before the war most Tynesiders were regular churchgoers. Religion influenced life in many ways, for instance through the Temperance Movement. Methodist churches in particular were strongly linked to Temperance, and it was never too early to persuade a child of the evils of alcohol. One Temperance Sunday, John T. recalls: 'We had a special service and on that day everybody was invited to sign the pledge. Even the children, anybody who wanted to, you know. We just signed it, I didn't know what it was.' Joe G. says, 'I remember signing the pledge at the age of six. A little boy in the school yard wanted to fight with me the next day and I said, "I can't, because I've signed the pledge." I thought it took away all pleasure!'

Many children found their Sundays taken up with a round of church services and Sunday school. Ted C. was brought up a Methodist in 1920s Jarrow. 'The church was very much my life. We used to go to

The Reverend Wakinshaw and a group of adults and children pose in front of Westerhope Methodist Church, Westerhope, 1923. (Courtesy of Newcastle Libraries Local Studies collection)

Members of Sunderland Sunday School's Union pose with the Examination Challenge Shield.

Sunday school, go to church three times on a Sunday, midweek and other services.' Elsie B. was taken to see a travelling boy preacher, entering Howard Hall[21] 'holding my father and mothers hand. We walked in and got a seat downstairs, there was sort of a platform, and the boy was there. I was just a kid, I wasn't interested much. He started to talk about the great salvation. I was only a kid, I was just listening, but I remember the text because my father wrote it down, he was an awful fellow for writing things down, he used to read them over and over again. Everybody was talking about it at the time.'

---

21 Howard Hall in North Shields started life as a Methodist chapel. It became
    a theatre in 1891, a few years before Elsie was born, but clearly maintained
    an association with Methodism. In 1908 it became a cinema, and showed
    so many Westerns that it quickly gained the nickname 'The Ranch'.

John T.'s Sunday school lessons in 1920s Gateshead sound very dull. 'We all had Bibles, with tiny print which you could hardly see, and we used to read round the class. What we used to do was count how many verses till yours, and just not listen 'til it got to yours.' Joan C. had a bit more fun, perhaps because she was only 3 when she started Sunday school in Newcastle in 1936. 'I remember making little flat roofed square houses out of paper. And there were sand trays, you used to make the desert with camels and things like that.'

Another attraction of some Sunday schools, especially before cinema, was the lantern slide show. Mr R. recalls that in the early 1900s 'in winter there was the lantern service on the Sunday night. There was a chap called Strong, a ship chandler on the Side in Newcastle, he had this huge lantern and he used to give lantern services. The Sunday school, it was a ha'penny to get in. We would go round and collect jam jars, they were all earthenware then you know. There was ha'pennies on them, so if we had one or two of them to take back to the Newcastle Tea Company we were well in, we were wealthy. And if we hadn't a ha'penny we'd run a chance, wait till the thing started, and chuck a little pebble in the basin with the ha'pennies. It used to work!'

Sunday school brought its own calendar of events. Mrs E.A. remembers that in the 1910s, South Shields would hold a Good Friday rally. 'We all used to gather at the top of Green Street, all the different churches from round about and we all marched down to the market and there was a half hour service there. Then we used to go back to the chapel and we used to have a service there. Then each child got an orange.' Joan C.'s Newcastle Sunday school held a 'flower service when children brought flowers', in June, and a Christmas service.

John T.'s Sunday school also held a Christmas party, with 'girls in their party frocks, boys in their best shirts. We had games and a good feed and then Santa Claus used to come and give everybody a present.' But for him and many others perhaps the biggest event of the year was the Anniversary. 'A special speaker used to sit in the pulpit, used to give an address in the middle of it and we in our best bib and tuckers, we used to recite and sing. One year I sang a solo, that was a red letter day, that!'

As well as Sunday school, boys with a good singing voice might find

The choir of St Michael's church, Newburn. (Courtesy of Newcastle Libraries Local Studies collection)

themselves entering the parish choir. John T. had a relaxed attitude. 'We used to pull faces in the back row. There was one night, my friend had just become the proud possessor of an electric torch. And the choir sang its anthem, "Send out thy Light". Well, you can imagine the light was shining from the back row. We got into serious trouble for that. The church steward wondered why the sopranos were laughing!'

Other choirs were more serious. Collinson B. made it through an audition to join the choir of St Nicholas Cathedral, Newcastle, in 1944. This was a large commitment, with a probationary period, rehearsals most evenings, and frequent performances. 'The discipline imposed by the head boy and the corner boys was tough. And the rigorous discipline of rehearsal was tremendous.'[22] The choir became his life. 'We were also paid a salary, we were professionals. We were not allowed to join the

---

22 Corner boys here are assistants to the head boy (although the word more commonly means someone who lounges around on street corners!).

Scouts, the Cadets – the choir was everything. We were not required to do homework, much to the fury of the masters at Dame Allan's. We were a law unto ourselves.'

Six

In the Wars

The Boer War

Some of the oldest of our interviewees can take us back as far as the Boer War (1899–1902). Nancy Y. was only a few years old at the time, but said, 'One morning we were in school singing "Above the Bright Blue Skies", and suddenly we heard a band play. The teacher stopped the hymn and said we could look out the window. There were soldiers marching down Barrack Road. It was the Elswick Battery walking off to the Boer War. And the teacher said, "Some of them might never come back. It'll be a long time before they reach South Africa, I hope the war's over before they get there."'[23]

The Boer War did not cause as much disruption at home as the great wars of the twentieth century. But victories were celebrated with bonfires,

23 Elswick Battery were unusual. In 1900 generally only infantry and yeomanry
   volunteer units were being formed, not batteries. But an exception was made
   for the 1st Northumberland Royal Garrison Artillery volunteers, who raised a
   battery for the war almost entirely made up of men from Elswick Ordnance Works.
   This made them probably the only men in the field to be armed with field
   guns they made themselves! The battery existed for around eighteen months,
   saw considerable enemy action and won several medals – but amazingly,
   Nancy Y.'s teacher had her wish, and none of its members were killed.

This boy's 'African' fancy dress is clearly inspired by the Boer War *(c.* 1900).

often with a stuffed figure like a guy on top. Mr C.R. of Gateshead was 3 years old during the Relief of Ladysmith (1900). 'My mother's sister was a dressmaker. And my Uncle Jack gave away her tailor's dummy to make a Kruger with, to burn on the fire. Aunt was mad you know!'[24]

The Relief of Mafeking a few months later was another cause for celebration. Nancy Y. remembers: 'They made a great big bonfire in the middle of the Barrack Square.[25] Those that could afford it went and bought new buckets, and got them filled with beer at the Darnell. They brought it down to drink when the bonfire was lit. At night-time my parents said, "Now stay in bed, because we're going to have a look at the bonfire." We heard our parents go out. And then I saw the flash of red in the sky, and I said to my little brother, "Come on Jimmy, we'll go and see the bonfire" – so off we went in our nightclothes. There was a great blaze, and people dancing round the bonfire. When the bonfire looked like going out they went into their houses and brought some more of their furniture out and piled it on. Just at that moment, our parents found us on the outskirts of the crowd. We got a clout each and got taken back home!'

----------------- *The First World War* -----------------

The First World War had massive effects on day-to-day life. Assuming their relatives did not sign up – and many thousands did – children would perhaps first have noticed the change at their schools, with male teachers being replaced by women, the old, young and disabled, those not fit for war service. To add to that, soldiers were often stationed in schools. Richard C. was aiming for a prize watch, for four years good attendance, when war broke out, and remembers 'every so often a batch of soldiers would come in for two or three days and maybe you'd get an afternoon at school. That was no good.

24 Paul Kruger was a figurehead of the Boers, at that time living
     in Holland and vigorously promoting the Boer cause.
25 Barrack Square was a block of housing forming three sides
     of a square, where New Mills meets Barrack Road.

At a butchers shop in Elisabethville, Birtley, a group of girls draw their families'
meat rations, *c.* 1915.

So after that I thought "I'll not get my watch now" so I used to
dodge school!'

Tom B. shared South Street School, Gateshead, with soldiers.
'The girls went half the day, we went the other half. The services were
billeted in the girls' part and there was a wall with a railing on top.
So of course, I was curious. I was looking over, and for some reason
I slipped. My head went through the railings and I jammed! I can
remember the soldiers had to hold us to the top of the railings, and the
mason had to chip the stone away, till they got us out.'

More seriously, the east coast was first in line of fire for enemy attack.
Tyneside and Wearside escaped the bombardment from German
warships which caused havoc in Hartlepool in December 1914, but
the area was a tempting target for Zeppelins. Peter T. remembers this
leading to a largely forgotten blackout. He says, 'Everybody had a
luminous button at night time they used to put it in their coat, it was
about the size of a twopenny piece, and you used to see them in the
dark and when you went down Gateshead High Street in the dark, all
you could see was buttons.'

Thelma W., aged 10, was looking out of her window in Whitley Bay,
when 'I just looked up and there was this great Zeppelin. And it seemed
to open this trap door and a ray of light came down, and that must have

been when the bomb dropped.'[26] Mrs C. says, perhaps of the same raid, 'It was a Sunday, we went down to see what had happened, everybody was going down to see this, and there wasn't a single pane of glass in Whitley Bay station. There's a lot of glass, the way it's built, but there wasn't a single one left. This was caused by a Zeppelin raid.'

When the bombs fell, there wasn't much you could do. Mrs C. continues, 'The South Shields raid, I remember the noise of it happening during the night. The lights went out, you didn't have a siren; the lights flickered to tell you something was going on, tell you to get into the room. Then the lights went out completely, I can't remember torches or anything, we had nightlights for the baby and candles of course. My baby sister and I were put underneath the kitchen table to sleep, with cushions, covered up with a rug, you had to just settle down, at least you were protected by the table.' Mr M. remembers a neighbour's comically unsuccessful attempt to prepare for Zeppelin attack. 'They were practicing for when the Germans came. There was a chest of drawers, and George got in the drawer, and they closed it up – and it hadn't any knobs on to pull it open! They couldn't get him out, they couldn't get the drawer out. They couldn't get their fingers in. They got what we used to call a gully, a carving knife, just so they could ease it out. But that was where he was going to get if the Germans had come.'

No wonder people pushed the boat out when the Armistice was declared. Margaret H. of Prudhoe was only 4 at the time, and her earliest memory is that 'everybody's tables was brought out and lovely white clothes put on. Everything was homemade and it was beautiful. We had earth toilets, middens that you put your ashes in, from the coal fires. I remember all that was covered with branches from the tree, greenery. The boys had covered it all, everything was decorated.'

But the conflict was not easily forgotten. Mr P.J., born in 1918, believes that he 'grew up in the shadow of the Great War, at a time when there

---

26 Four Zeppelin raids targeted the Tyne and Wear area in 1915–16. Thelma W.
   is probably thinking of a raid which crossed South Shields, North Shields,
   Jarrow, Tynemouth and Whitley Bay in the early hours of 9 August 1916.
   A lot of glass was broken, but there were surprisingly few casualties.

A street party to celebrate the end of the First World War, Byker, 1918.

was still a British Empire. An Armistice service was held in the school hall at 11 a.m. on November the 11th. One of our masters in the senior school would break down and weep. When, in 1928, the Kellogg Pact was signed, we were assured in the school hall that there would never again be another war.'[27]

The Second World War – Evacuation

Mr P.J.'s teachers were sadly mistaken, and only eleven years later war broke out across Europe once more. Lives were turned upside down, as school, food, clothing, family, all life's most dependable features, were shaped by the needs of a nation at war. Emily K. was 13 when war was declared. That morning, she'd been roped in by her grandfather,

---

27 The Kellogg-Briand pact was also called the World Peace Act. It was signed by fifteen countries, who agreed that war was to be renounced as an instrument of national policy. It was, of course, unenforceable, and did little to prevent the conflicts of the next twenty years. However, it is still a binding treaty in international law, and helped establish the groundwork for international law on war, and the idea of a 'crime against peace'.

who owned a newsagents, to help deliver the Sunday papers. 'It was just turned eleven o'clock, that was when war was declared, I was knocking on this woman's door to give her her paper when the siren went. Well it was chaos, I didn't know which way to run, whether to run home or what to do. A man across the road, he opened his front door and he shouted to me to come in to his house. I went in, and he put me under the stairs with his own children and gave me his gas mask. And I never forgot that man for that. He had took me into his home and there's me huddled under the stairs with this man's gas mask. That was the Sunday morning that the war started.'

Thousands of children were sent away from the region as evacuees, often to the Lake District or the more remote valleys of western Northumberland and Durham, strange and unfamiliar landscapes to city kids. Some learned to milk cows, or look after newborn lambs. Even other towns had their own personality. Joe G. remembers: 'We arrived at Wigton, and the first thing that hit me was the most dreadful smell of rotten eggs. There was a factory there made a kind of cellophane called rayophane, and this smell hung over the town.'[28]

Evacuation was not always an easy choice. Joan W.'s family were divided on whether to send 7-year-old Joan away from Byker to Middleton-in-Teesdale, and she says, 'It must have been terrible for mother, to let two children go. She told me years later that her sisters and brothers and parents weren't very happy, and they didn't speak to her for three days afterwards.'

Some boys and girls took the whole thing in their stride. Harry W. saw it as 'a great big adventure. In the first place, I'd never been on a train before.' Twelve-year-old Joe G. was less keen. 'I waved my brother goodbye, and got on a train with the heaviest heart I think I've ever had in my life before or since. The other kids were all playing, and they all seemed to know each other. I found out later they didn't, they were just a little bit more outgoing than me.'

---

28 Wigton is a small Cumbrian market town to the west of Carlisle. British New Wrap Co. Ltd began making cellulose film there in 1934. Two years later the company started making rayon (optimistically called 'artificial silk'), an early artificial fabric a bit like nylon, and also rayophane (which is indeed cellophane). At this point it changed its name to British Rayophane Limited.

Meeting your new 'family' could be tough. Peg H. was sent to Culgaith, near Penrith. She says, 'You sat there with your little badge on your coat. My parents had dyed a pillowcase at the time, dark brown, to put my bits and pieces in, and my gas mask. And the vicar came, and he took me, and I thought, "Ee, I'll have to be a good girl all the time!" But he was taking me for the people I stayed with, because they couldn't come. And I remember thinking "Ee, thank goodness for that!"' Mr A.I., a Jewish boy who had recently come over from Germany, understandably found the whole experience of evacuation traumatic. He was sent to Carlisle, and 'when the hostess collected us, the first thing I said to her was "you know we are German Jews?" They probably had never seen a Jew in their life.' Things were particularly hard as he attempted to keep kosher: 'They couldn't understand why on earth I didn't want a glass of milk after I'd eaten meat, why I didn't want to eat different types of meat and things like that. It was very difficult.'

The *Durham Advertiser* photographed this group of evacuees arriving at Sherburn from Gateshead and Tynemouth, a few days after the outbreak of war, 1939. The children each carry a gas mask and wear an identity label.

Country life was very different. John C., sent from Jarrow to Lumley in County Durham, thought it was 'a totally different world. We had free range of the farms, the kids. We went tatey picking, and that was an eye-opener, 'cause in the winter, you had just a sack tied round your waist for to hold the tateys while you were picking them, and your hands like blocks of ice.'

But many children adapted to their new way of life, especially if they stayed away a long time. Peg H. ended up not in a vicarage but at 'a little smallholding kind of place, and we used to have to go to school on the sledge. It was great as kids, we thought it was wonderful.' Harry W., evacuated first to Kirklington and then Crakehall (both in North Yorkshire), says, 'I had to reintegrate with the Sunderland lads. I was a little Yorkshire lad when I came back.'

But the last laugh goes to Robert W. He was evacuated to Eslington Hall, near Whittingham, Northumberland, while his own Newcastle home became an officer's mess: 'So Lord Ravensworth was living in my house and I was living in his house!'

These two girls were evacuated from South Shields to the house of professional photographer J. Hardman of Kendal, who proceeded to use them as models for a series of images. Here, they watch the sheep shearing.

─────────────── *Air Raids* ───────────────

Whether at home or away, you couldn't get away from the war, and that meant the air raids. Elizabeth M.'s mother brought the family back from evacuation after a raid, reasoning that 'if we're going to get killed, we're all going to get killed together.' Betty S.'s mother used almost exactly the same words to justify not sending her daughter away at all. But while her school remained open, for a handful of pupils, the schools in Elizabeth M.'s corner of Gateshead had closed. 'They started a series of house schools. People would give their front room and the teachers would go and teach. I went to one in Howard Street, but there was an air raid and those two houses were destroyed. And then after that there was an arrangement come to with King Edward School that we went to school half days.'

In Newcastle the bombing continued. Jack H. was taking the family's accumulator batteries to be topped up one evening when he had a close encounter with a bomber in the streets of South Benwell. 'Suddenly this plane come along and went "hu-hu-hu-hu-hu" and I thought "My God, where's that come from?" It was machine-gun fire! The sirens hadn't gone. This bomber had crept in unnoticed, unseen. I took to my heels and I was away home.' Collinson B. saw the same plane, which ended up dropping a bomb on the massive Spillers Mill, Newcastle. 'The chap in the nose was taking pot shots at anything that moved, a dog or whatever. And he saw us. My grandfather pulled me around the corner, out of sight of this aeroplane, which was very low. We could see the crosses on the grey underside, as close as anything, droning over.'

No wonder the blackout was kept so carefully. Elizabeth M., now 13 and studying at a commercial college, recalls that 'coming home in the blackout was a nightmare. You had to walk along Sunderland Road, in Gateshead, because by then the trams stopped. Sometimes you were lucky and caught the last one, but not always. One night the tram was coming and I ran for it, and ran full force into a lamp post! And broke three ribs!'

Air-raid shelters too became part of everyday life. Joan W.'s grandfather ruled over a household of women and children. 'No one was allowed to sleep outside that house during the night, they all had to be under the same roof so he could be in charge of them! And see that they were in the shelter. We would all be ushered into the shelter in the garden. Then if we were very lucky, grandfather would go out and make cocoa for us. That was a luxury, with the sugar and the chocolate, it was lovely. My grandmother kept it especially for the shelter, that was a treat.' She continues, 'My aunty had a little girl, and she was put into a great big enormous gas mask, she went right into it, and they zipped her up in this gas mask, which terrified me. When you were going into the shelter you could see the searchlights and the Ack Ack going and the lights and the bombs and when you came back out you could see fires all over.'

Collinson B., too, remembers waiting for bombs to fall over Newcastle, listening to 'the din of the Ack Ack battery up the block, and the barrage balloons during the daytime, and bombers at night droning over and their bombs coming down. Several times they were

George Street, North Shields, in May 1941, shortly after an air raid. (Tyneside Planning Department collection)

so close, I was sitting inside the shelter and watching the flash of the bomb through the shelter door – which was well screened off by heavy sandbags – and the whole thing was rocking. We were always convinced the house had had a direct hit. We'd walk a street or two away and find a block of houses smashed to pieces the next day, that was how close it got.'

There was one upside to the situation, as Jack H. explains: 'We were getting the air raids then almost every night. Now if the raid lasted over an hour, after midnight, you didn't have to go to school, they let you have a long lie-in, so of course we were sitting thinking, "Another five minutes, don't let the all clear go". And very often we just said, "Ee well, I'm sure it was an hour", and we didn't go to school. And they said, "It wasn't an hour", and we got wrong!'

Freedom and Responsibility

With adults preoccupied, older boys took on more responsibility. Jack H. was not evacuated with most of his friends, so he had no school at all for months, and then only a few hours a day. 'I was twelve then and strongish, so I took over an allotment. I got hens, and there was one or two fellows had the allotments there got called up, so I took over three allotments. I used to dig for victory. I used to grow rhubarb and lettuce, and sell it to the corner shop.' Girls too might gain extra responsibilities. Betty S. was often given the ration book. 'At the top of the street used to be a fruit shop and if we knew there was any fruit, with me being the oldest she [mother] used to send me up to stand in the queue.'

Collinson B., five years younger than Jack H., was left to his own devices, and made the most of it. He especially enjoyed collecting militaria. 'Every day after the air raid, you were out straight away on your bike hunting for the shrapnel. Particularly attractive were the tail fins of the incendiary bombs, these were circular things with a cross fin in them. Those were great for swapping. Also we'd chase around after the barrage balloons that had broken their moorings, they would fly through the air, and again, they were dangerous. One untoward flame

A large house with garden is being used as a nursery school (*c.* 1940). Here the children wave Union Flags. (Courtesy of Newcastle Libraries Local Studies collection)

or spark, if they caught on the tram lines or something like that, they would go off bang. When they had been deflated we used to try and get hold of the barrage balloon material, this silvery stuff, quite tough. That was highly prized.'

Joan W. was the same age as Collinson B., but lived a very different life in the bosom of her extended family. She enjoyed visits home by uncles in military service, and listened to the radio for news. 'You had the radio on all the time to listen to what was happening. And at one time it was so bad, there was awful news all the time, there was no hope in sight. Then the allies were starting to win, and I used to say to mam, "Mam, how many aircraft were shot down last night?" and "How many Germans were killed?" And she used to say, "Now remember in Germany there will be mothers and sisters and aunts and uncles crying about those, just like we cried about Bobby and Geordie. They're somebody's bairns." And this has taken me right through my life, they're somebody's bairns.'

Still, she remembers the victory celebration with fondness. 'We had a party in the street with tables right out, two blocks in the street. We had great bonfires, there was lots of servicemen there, lots of dancing. The thing I remember the most is the next morning, where the bonfire had broken all the road up and everything was all cracked – it had done the same damage as the bombs did!'

Seven

Harsh Reality

Poverty Knocks

Tyneside's big industrial workforces have long been vulnerable to shifts in the economy, and even at the best of times there were some that fell into dire poverty. If your father was unemployed or had a low-paid job, or if you had lots of brothers and sisters, it was hard to make the money stretch to cover the basics. Mothers might go hungry to make sure the children had enough, and treats were very rare. Joseph F., who was born in Rowland's Gill in 1904, recalls that 'as time got on, things was getting worse, and we were lucky for survival. As the saying was, them days, money wasn't easy to get. Of course, we got through ... but it was hard on the parents.'

It didn't help that, before the mass slum clearances of the 1930s, some areas of Tyneside were graced with truly shocking housing stock. In 1932, 4-year-old Alan C.'s family moved to a tenement in Felling. 'This place was so filthy that the bed bugs were crawling up the wall, the place was vile, so vile we could hardly live in it. We had to get a sanitary inspector in to smoke each room out with sulphur candles in an effort to get the livestock down. And I suppose we felt we'd sunk as low as we could possibly sink.'

Alan C.'s lot was not unusual. As the region's industries went from boom to bust in the 1920s and '30s, many men struggled to provide for their families. Jean R. was a child in 1920s Jarrow, and watched as her unemployed father, one of thousands of men in a similar situation, headed to the docks every morning to look for temporary work, queuing up in the hope of a few hours labour. 'He used to go out every morning and get us up for school when he come back, no jobs.' Some men even went to the workhouse each day, where they broke stones in exchange for food tickets.

Things picked up a bit when Britain's industries were regenerated by the prospect of war, but this didn't reach everyone. In 1938, Mr A.I., a 10 year old fleeing Hitler's Germany, saw his new home town with the eyes of an outsider, and was shocked. 'It was a depressing place. I still remember the sight of the children walking around in bare feet with just a shirt on, mother wheeling a filthy pram full of coal. The houses were depressing, to put it mildly.'

To help families through tough times, anything they owned might find its way to the pawn shop to be redeemed when it was needed again. Even fairly respectable families might pawn Sunday-best clothes on Monday, and get them back for the Sunday church service, just to have a little more cash available in the week. But it was often a cause of shame. In the mid-1930s,

Children queue for food at a South Shields soup kitchen, 1918.

Joe G.'s mother sent him to a Newcastle pawn shop every week to pawn his father's Sunday-best suit (without his father's knowledge). One week he forgot to collect it, and when his father found out he was mortified.

Poverty crept into every corner of life. For instance, fathers often got no pay for the Christmas break, and found it hard to save enough to get by for that time, let alone buy presents. Joe G. remembers that shops in Newcastle 'would suddenly have a whole lot of toys on display, toys which I knew I would never get, I used to just stand there looking at them with very envious eyes'. As Joseph F. explains, 'We appreciated anything we got – we didn't get much, but we loved it. You maybe just got one thing in your stocking, some oranges and apples and nuts.'

At least his parents cared enough to try. For others, poverty went hand-in-hand with neglect. John L. (born in Newcastle in 1892) was given a suit of clothing by his grandfather, who was a tailor. 'I wore it once, brought it home, put it in the drawer and that was the last I seen of it. Everything we had was taken out and put in the pawn shop. My mother was what you would now call an alcoholic, and it didn't matter what it was, she would have it. Home life was very poor. You could go home, and nine times out of ten your mother wasn't in, she was in the public house at the corner of Prudhoe Street and Percy Street, and that went on, day, day and every day.' He'd never met his father, and his mother lived with 'a man called Black. I was known as John Black for years. And – just before the war broke out, I found out my name was really something else. He was a bit of an alcoholic as well.'

Hunger could drive children like John L. to desperate measures. He would hang around Newcastle Green Market, then a vegetable market opposite St Andrew's church. 'We used to spend our time pinching a bit of cabbage here, something else there, and carrots. It was on the ground, you see.' According to Alan L., children waited on the Fish Quay in the 1920s and picked up any herring which had fallen onto the dockside – the fish would be taken home and salted in barrels in the back yard. And in Jarrow, Jean R.'s friends stole from the Ormonde Street shops. 'They stole eggs and that and used to bring them home. Or steal them and sell them.'

Or you could simply beg. Thomas G. remembers that in the streets of Depression-era Gateshead, children 'used to stand waiting outside the

Three boys stare into a shop window on Bottle Bank, Gateshead.

On the Fish Quay (*c.* 1910), a fish sorter poses with a group of lads.

factory gates asking "Any bait, mister?" from men what's coming out of work, asking if they had any bread and butter or a bit of sandwich left.' Nancy Y. agrees, remembering that when 'the buzzer went at half past eight, there were little children, hardly school age, standing with no stockings or shoes on and they used to say, "Any left? Any left? Any left?" And the men, if they had a sandwich left, a bit of bread left, saved it for those children and that was their breakfast.'

Food wasn't the only thing that could disappear, and petty theft could become an important part of balancing the domestic budget. In the 1930s, Sunderland lads Les S. and Jim G. found a windfall on the railway tracks. 'In them days they used to shunt coal from one place to another. There used to be loads and loads off the tracks, we would retrieve that and sling it over the wall and we used to take it home. When we took it home it was essential. We still used to get a clip.'

In the face of this poverty, there were sporadic – and sometimes rather odd – attempts to improve children's lot. Joe G. recalls his teacher saying, '"all those children whose daddies are not working, stand on the seat" – and of course the children stood and they were given small packets of giveaway wheat flakes. And I remember feeling deprived that I couldn't have one – my father was in a job.' Mr A. remembers 'the great Daddy Bowran, Bowran's Mission, who on Easter morning gave away as many eggs as must have been laid in Denmark that week! Children queued up with tickets to get boiled eggs for Easter.'[29]

Sometimes, too, things were free or cheap for all those willing to wait – which usually meant it was a chore for the kids. Margaret R. (born in Willington Quay in 1916) hated queuing for free wood at Clennel's ship repair yard on a Saturday morning, 'but it saved a lot of money. And every second or third week we used to queue again with a two-pound sugar bag for monkey nuts. They used to give wor them free.' Then there was 'Lowries egg factory – where you could go down with as big a jar as possible and get it filled with cracked eggs for a penny – and the kippering houses

29 Methodist George Bowran founded the Prudhoe Street Mission
    in 1910. It gave away a lot more than eggs – in 1925 it distributed
    52,000 meals and another 10,000 bowls of soup, and gave
    temporary shelter to around 11,000 homeless men.

under Byker bridge. At five minutes to five, just before they were closing they would collect all the kippers that had fallen off the smoking rails, and sell them to anybody for a penny,' recalls Mr A.[30]

Bare Feet and Charity Shoes

If food was hard to come by, clothing and footwear were more so. Nancy Y. remembers children in Edwardian Newcastle 'walking about in the snow in bare feet ... I've seen children with their fathers' old jackets on and nothing else.' For the poorest, clothes would be bought second-hand – perhaps at Paddy's Market, held on Saturdays on the Quayside, which specialised in old clothes – patched, remade, passed on, and reused as rags. Even for those with more money, clothing would be made to last, and as Joan W. explains, 'Most of the stuff was sort of handed down, or if you had something and outgrew it, you'd give it to Mrs So-and-so 'cause she's got a lot of bairns.'

Being raggedly dressed and barefoot marked you out, and children can be cruel, as Elizabeth K. found out at High West Street School, Gateshead, around the time of the First World War. 'I had bare feet, and on the schoolyard were stones, little stones. And when we used to play games the girls wouldn't take my hand. Well that used to hurt me. 'Cause you see a lot of girls were nicely dressed, had better bringings-up.'

Perhaps this is why the best remembered form of charity for children came in the form of shoes – often marked to prevent resale or pawning – donated by schemes set up by companies, the police, the Salvation Army and more. Nancy Y. thinks that 'the First World War, if it didn't bring a peace on earth, it brought a little bit of comfort to those children because they then had boot and shoe clubs, they could go and get boots and shoes.' But they were a mixed blessing. For a start they were almost as obvious a marker of poverty as bare feet. Joe G.'s friend, at Todd's Nook school in the 1920s, 'was beaten up

---

30 Based in Byker, Lowrie Foods have been trading for over

   100 years, and specialising in eggs for most of that time.

by the other boys in the class because he'd let the school down by accepting Lord Mayor's boots.'

Then there were quality problems. Mrs E.S., who grew up in Edwardian Sunderland, says, 'They were laced, they were so cheap the eyelet holes of the brass used to shine. And they were so hard up against the flesh that the mammies had to cut them, for them to give around the ankles.' Her contemporary, William C. of Whickham was also given some scheme shoes. 'They sometimes used to send a pair of shoes that were much too big by half. You were crippled with them. I remember my sister carrying me to school on her back, to get me to school. You were all right once you got into the classroom.'

In summer, at least, it might be easier to just take the boots off – and your friends would join you. Wallsend lad Richard C. preferred to go without, to the discomfort of his father (who had, after all, spent good money on shoes). 'Often I would run out without them just to be the same as the other lads. My father would play war – "You've got a pair of shoes, you're not wearing them." I was quite happy running around in my bare feet.' Ernie K. also ran around with his shoeless friends on the streets of 1920s South Shields, saying, 'You used to get

---

THE BOROUGH OF TYNEMOUTH

Isaac Black Boot & Shoe Fund

To Messrs. D. Hill, Carter & Co., Ltd.,

Union Street, North Shields.

Please supply Bearer with a Pair of Boots

and Stockings for a BOY/GIRL age   years and

charge to this Fund.

T. BLACKBURN,

Hon. Administrator.

Ticket issued in 1941 by the Chief Constable of Tynemouth as representative of a Boot and Shoe Fund.

tar off the roads on your feet, and your mother used to rub butter on your feet to get it off.'

In Style

Whether they wore them or not, most children would have boots for everyday wear and sand shoes for summer. As Ernie K. says, he and his friends 'wore sand shoes, plimsolls, they were about a shilling a pair. They used to last about a fortnight and you had to get another pair – 'cause you were out running!'

A more hard-wearing option was clogs. Thomas G. had wooden clogs with iron hoops on the bottom, bought from a clog shop on Castle Garth Stairs, Newcastle, around the time of the First World War. He remembers: 'You could run down the main street and slide in them.' Elizabeth A., a few years older, remembers a clog man on Carr Stairs, Newcastle. 'There was a little room, and there was an old gentleman lived in there and he used to make wooden clogs. I used to love to sit and watch him cut the clogs, all sizes, little ones, big ones. I used to think it was marvellous! Oh and he used to paint them, varnish them, and oh we had something lively, it was nice.'

While some clothing was shop bought, many women could make, or at least alter children's clothing. In the 1910s, Margaret R.'s mother shopped at Fosters, a Wallsend drapers. 'They used to sell tweed, five pence a yard, so you know what happened, us five sisters always had the same tweed things on!' Joan W.'s mother enlisted her sister's friend's help. 'They used to take old dresses to pieces. I think if I had five dresses you were very well off.' Mr T.G. wore corduroy suits, and his mother 'used to knit socks and shorts and vests'.

Whether bought or made, children's clothing was often a miniature version of the elaborate adult clothing of the time. In the 1910s, Mrs B. 'went to school in white silk blouses that we got at the Copenhagen in Grey Street for ten and sixpence. And we always went in clean white pinafores. And silk stockings!' During the Second World War, Joan W. wore 'a pinafore dress and a jumper, and long stockings in the winter, long stockings that used to drive me crazy. Woollen things were terrible

Thelma W. and her sister, taken at Whitley Bay (*c.* 1915).

in those days, scratching them and crying. Mam would say, "You've got to wear them, it's too cold not to wear them."'

And of course underwear, even for children, was far more substantial back then. When Elizabeth M. remembers 1930s clothing, her first thought is of 'liberty bodices, horrible, horrible, vests and liberty bodices. And petticoats, full petticoats.'

For a girl, hair was also important. Nancy L.'s Edwardian mother was very choosy. 'My mother would never let us have our hair in plaits, we used to think "I wish we could have our hair in plaits", but we all had ringlets.'

Until Edwardian times, many small boys spent their first few years wearing dresses similar to those of their sisters. As they got older they were 'breeched'. Joseph F. went into 'little short buttoned cords, they were the main trousers. They had buttons that fastened below the knee, and they were quite warm. Then there was a dark blue jersey, a rubber collar, and my cap. And you had a little overcoat.' Collars were particularly important. They were often rubber so as to be easily washable – or you could cheat. Rebecca B. remembers class photographs at Prior Street School, Nun's Lane, Newcastle, in the 1910s. 'When we got our photos taken, some boys would be in their bare feet, but the teacher would get an exercise book and make paper collars. You would never think they had a paper collar on when they got their photo took.'

———————— *Making a Few Coppers* ————————

No wonder as soon as they could run, some boys were looking for ways to make a penny, either for themselves or more often to chip into the family pot. This might start out as just message running, but some, like Thomas G. of Gateshead, got more creative. 'If anybody wanted their dog put down, or their cat, I used to take them to the slaughterhouse and I used to get a few coppers. Aye, and messages and that, and flour. If anyone wanted half a stone of flour from the Co-operative, they'd give you a pillow-slip and you used to get it in a pillow-slip.' Not that the gain was always in coin – when Dorothy S. ran messages, 'you didn't get money, you got a biscuit or a tatey or something like that shoved in your hand.'

Group of children in Sandgate, 1898. One is carrying firewood, to take home or perhaps to sell. (Courtesy of Newcastle Libraries Local Studies collection)

On the streets of Newcastle there were lots of odd jobs for an enterprising lad. In the late 1930s, Joe G. would exchange rags for coppers in a rag shop on Heber Street, and sell wood. 'We would occasionally go down to Newcastle market with a barrow. We would get empty boxes, take them back, chop them up, bundle them and sell them to the local traders, or go round the doors with them, selling them.' In Sunderland, Les S. and Jim G. had similar ideas. 'We made a bay for ourselves near the water, by the launch of Deptford shipyard, we used to go in there swimming. All the wood we used to bring in, we used to dry it out, cut it, chop it up into sticks and distribute it round all the people. Some used to give us a penny, which was not bad in them days.'

John L., who we met a moment ago stealing carrots to supplement what little he got from an alcoholic mother, was also happy to work. 'In those days the *Chronicle* was only a halfpenny and you could go down to the *Chronicle* office and get three *Chronicles* for a penny. Well, if you sold the three you made a halfpenny profit, and I used to do that. And I used to stand at Samuels, in Newgate Street, and sell my papers, and get chased by the police. Because you shouldn't have been standing there, you see, you had to be on the move all the time.'

A lad sells newspapers on Grainger Street (*c.* 1898). (Courtesy of Newcastle Libraries Local Studies collection)

Shop Boys and Delivery Carts

Various shops would take young lads as employees – for instance, in 1922 John H. worked in a barbers at 11 years old, and part-time work with a butcher seems to have been quite common. Roderick A. was also 11 in 1917, when he began to work in a Newcastle butchers. He worked 'after school from four o'clock till seven, skinning rabbits, and fowls. Kippers came in big barrels, about twelve stone, and they were frozen in there. I'd set them on the slab so they were thawed for the morning. The rabbits were Australian rabbits, and we would pare them, hang them up and put sawdust on the ground and they used to drip till the next day, then we used to skin them.'[31]

He continues, 'I went in every morning seven o'clock, except Sundays, and finished at quarter to nine. School was only five minutes away. It was a very busy life. I had a cap I wore at work, but I used to always leave it, and a blue-and-white striped apron that covered me right over. I got very washed before I went to school, but there was always a faint poultry smell. The school authorities didn't like it but as long as your homework was done, and you didn't fall asleep, it was OK.'

It was a similar story for Gateshead lad Mr C.R., who in 1907 managed to combine school work with work for a butcher and a newsagent. 'On Friday night I worked in the butchers till eleven o'clock. Saturday it was papers, get my breakfast, then the butchers till dinner time, deliver some papers, back to the butchers, then at two o'clock I'd deliver for two hours. Back to the butchers, get my tea, deliver papers, back to the butchers, and I've seen me on the Quayside carrying meat to the corner store at one in the morning. And I was only 10.'

If a relative owned a business, you would soon get roped in. Ernie K.'s family ran a wherry boat on the Tyne, and he could be called upon at any time. 'My father used to keep me off school, before I finished, if they were busy on the river diving he would take me away from school.' Norman A.'s father was a North Shields greengrocer and in 1923, aged 11, 'I was an errand boy, I carried the orders all round. We had

31 In Australia at this time the rabbit population was exploding (reaching a peak of 10 billion in 1926). One response to this glut was extermination and export.

This group of abattoir workers includes two boys.

to take them out on a little wooden barrow, which was beautifully hand painted, green and cream and red and things. In about a year he let me serve outside the window and then gave me a job after about a few months to stand outside the big shop next to the Theatre Royal in Prudhoe Street, North Shields. You used to have to stand there winter and summer, snow, rain, anything, they'd pull the sun shade out. You used to be allowed in for your meal, it used to be six slices of bread and two hard-boiled eggs. At nine o'clock me father used to say, "It's late enough for a young lad to be here", and I was sent home with a bag of fruit like everybody else.'

Delivery work was common. In 1915, 12-year-old Charles D. of Sunderland spent his Saturdays working a twelve-hour shift, driving a horse with a coal wagon for a shilling. Around 1918, Tom B. had a milk round. 'You had a churn on a kind of trap. Before I went to school I used to get the little gallon can, the dipper, and I used to go right the way down Cranbourne Road, and get the jug on the step, tip a bit in. For that I used to get half a crown a week and a packet of sweets.' He also helped an illiterate man deliver sweets. 'He didn't know what to deliver, you see, from the sheets. And you had to read them to the old lady shopkeepers because half them couldn't read them either.'

A delivery boy from Maypole Dairy, Newcastle, stands with his milk cart (*c.* 1920).

Other more unusual places also hired young lads. Jim B. lived near Birtley Golf Club, and was determined to make money from it. As a small boy he started off carrying grass cuttings around in exchange for free games. He was soon collecting balls and selling them back to players, for three pence each. He even kept notes to avoid selling one back to the man who'd lost it. In 1933, aged 9, he started work as a caddy, for sixpence a round. 'Twice the money I'd saved caddying got the family a week's holiday at Cullercoats.'

Twenty years earlier Bill also gained from living near a golf course – in this case, Ravensworth. His story shows just how important it might be to the family that a child went out to work. He remembers: 'Before I started at the quarry I used to go over Ravensworth golf course carrying for the golfers, while I was going to school. Every Saturday. And I got on carrying for a chap, Mr Nixon; he got me to wait every Saturday. He used to go once around, and I used to clean his clubs after the match you know, with emery paper. He would come out the golf house and say, "There's four shillings, take that home to your mother, and there's sixpence for yourself." Well out of that sixpence I could go to the pictures for tuppence, buy a bottle of pop for a penny, and get a three-ha'penny paper of fish and chips. I used to give my mother the four shillings on the Saturday, many a time. Talk about hard times, she was waiting on us coming back, and as soon as she got the four shillings she was away off to the butchers to get something to eat for the Sunday. I was the eldest of nine. Hard days.'

Moving On

But whatever the part-time work, the real thing soon beckoned. Girls might stay at home looking after siblings. Mrs B.C.'s teacher called her out of class at 12 years old, to tell her, '"You can leave school if you wish to. Do you wish to leave?" "Oh,"' I says, '"yes", because my mother hadn't anybody at home, and she had the two little ones.' Others might look for work, often in domestic service or as a shop assistant – though most girls would only expect to work until they married and began to have children of their own. Boys usually left school only a few days after their fourteenth birthday, not

A young lad ready for a day at work.

waiting for the academic year to turn around. Many stepped straight into jobs, often arranged by their fathers – like Mr M., who 'left school on the Friday and started work at the pit on the Monday.' And after they had left school, even though they still lived with their little brothers and sisters, they moved into a whole new world, with shifts and pay packets, football with other apprentices and starting to chase the girls. And with that, they move out of this book.

List of Contributors

My thanks go to all whose stories appear in this book:

Bill of Springwell, b. 1901
Mamie of Newcastle, b. 1901
Mary of Newcastle, b. 1912
Mr A. of Newcastle, b. unknown
Mrs A. of Newcastle, b. 1898
Mrs E.A. of South Shields, b. 1904
Ethel A. of Newcastle, b. 1903
Norman A. of North Shields, b. 1912
Roderick A. of Newcastle, b. 1905
Mrs B. of Newcastle, b. 1898
Collinson B. of Newcastle, b. 1932
Dennis B. of Newcastle, b. 1914
Elsie B. of North Shields, b. 1897
Ethel B. of South Shields, b. 1884
Jim B. of Birtley, b. 1924
Minnie B. of Willington, b. 1902
Mary Bl. of Newcastle, b. 1908
Mary Br. of Newcastle, b. 1902
Percy B. of Newburn, b. 1906
Rebecca B. of Gateshead, b. 1897
Tom B. of Gateshead, b. 1908
Alan C. of Washington, b. 1929
Mrs B.C. of Hebburn, b. 1877
Billie C. of Newcastle, b. 1923

Mrs C. of North Shields, b. 1910
Mr C. of Newcastle b. 1905
Mrs E.C. of Newcastle, b. 1898
Joan C. of Newcastle, b. 1933
John C. of Jarrow, b. 1930
Norah C. of Newcastle, b. 1900
Richard C. of Wallsend, b. 1905
Ted C. of Jarrow, b. 1918
William C. of Whickham, b. 1904
Charles D. of Sunderland, b. 1903
Elsie D. of Gateshead, b. 1922
Joseph D. of Gateshead, b. 1929
Reece E. of Birtley, b. 1895
Frank F. of Newcastle, b. 1902
Mr F. of Newcastle, b. 1909
George F. of Newcastle, b. *c.* 1910
Joseph F. of Rowlands Gill, b. 1904
Annie G. of Blanchland, b. 1912
Ella G. of Gateshead, b. 1909
Frank G. of Sunderland, b. 1913
Jim G. of Sunderland, b. 1926
Joe G. of Newcastle, b. 1927
Thomas G. of Gateshead, b. 1910
Horsley H. of Byker, b. 1915

John H. of Gateshead, b. 1911
Jack H. of Benwell, b. 1927
Margaret H. of Prudhoe, b. 1914
Peg H. of Benwell, b. 1927
Tom H. of Hetton-le-Hole, b. 1923
Mr A.I. of Gateshead, b. 1928
Mr P.J. of Newcastle, b. 1918
Peter J. of Newcastle, b. 1953
Ernie K. of South Shields, b. 1915
Elizabeth K. of Gateshead, b. 1909
Emily K. of South Shields, b. 1910
Henry K. of Newcastle, b. 1919
Tom K. of Seaton Carew, b. 1899
Alan L. of Tynemouth, b. 1913
John L. of Newcastle, b. 1892
Nan L. of Newcastle, b. 1909
Nancy L. of Newcastle, b. 1900
Elizabeth M. of Gateshead, b. 1928
Mr M. of Washington, b. 1910
Mary M. of Ryton, b. 1901
Margaret M. of Stamfordham, b. 1946
Elizabeth N. of Gateshead, b. 1891
Mr O. of Jesmond, b. 1906
Bella P. of Newcastle, b. 1910

George P. of Low Moorsley, b. 1915
Mr C.R. of Gateshead, b. 1897
Ethel R. of Gateshead, b. 1900
Gordon R. of Sunderland, b. 1922
Jack R. of Fencehouses, b. 1907
Jean R. of Jarrow, b. 1914
Margaret R. of Willington Quay, b. 1916
Mr M.R. of Newcastle, b. *c.* 1890
Mrs R. of Newcastle, b. unknown
Betty S. of Byker, b. unknown
Dorothy S. of Newcastle, b. unknown
Mrs E.S. of Sunderland, b. 1898
Miss J.S. of Sunderland, b. 1917
Les S. of Sunderland, b. 1939
John T. of Gateshead, b. 1917
Peter T. of Gateshead, b. 1908
Hannah W. of Denton, b. 1915
Harry W. of Sunderland, b. 1931
Joan W. of Byker, b. 1932
Robert W. of Newcastle, b. 1927
Thelma W. of Whitley Bay, b. 1908
Winifred W. of Newcastle, b. 1906
Nancy Y. of Newcastle, b. 1898

If you enjoyed this book, you may also be interested in ...

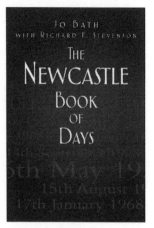

The Newcastle Book of Days

JO BATH AND RICHARD F. STEVENSON

Taking you through the year day by day, *The Newcastle Book of Days* contains quirky, eccentric, amusing and important events and facts from different periods in the history of the city. Ideal for dipping into, this addictive little book will keep you entertained and informed. Featuring hundreds of snippets of information gleaned from the vaults of Newcastle's archives and covering the social, criminal, political, religious, industrial, military and sporting history of the region, it will delight residents and visitors alike.

978 0 7524 6866 2

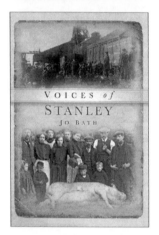

Voices of Stanley

JO BATH

This is a remarkable compilation of extracts drawn from the extensive Beamish Museum Oral History collection, recalling life in the area between 1880 and 1950. Vivid memories are recounted, including childhood and schooldays, work and play, sport and leisure, as well as the war years. It covers the harrowing search for bodies following the Stanley pit disaster of 1909 and lost sheep in the snows of 1947, as well as local traditions of possing, jarping and candymen. Richly illustrated with over seventy pictures from the museum archive, many previously unpublished, this volume paints a revealing picture of life in Stanley in years gone by.

978 0 7524 6037 6

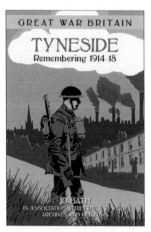

Great War Britain Tyneside: Remembering 1914–18

JO BATH IN ASSOCIATION WITH TYNE AND WEAR ARCHIVES AND MUSEUMS SERVICE

The First World War claimed over 995,000 British lives, and its legacy continues to be remembered today. *Great War Britain: Tyneside* offers an intimate portrayal of the city and its people living in the shadow of the 'war to end all wars'. A beautifully illustrated and highly accessible volume, it describes local reaction to the outbreak of war; charts the experience of individuals who enlisted; the changing face of industry and related unrest; the work of the many hospitals in the area; the effect of the conflict on local children; and concludes with a chapter dedicated to how the city and its people coped with the transition to life in peacetime once more.

978 0 7509 5651 2

Visit our website and discover thousands of other History Press books.

www.thehistorypress.co.uk

Printed in Great Britain
by Amazon.co.uk, Ltd.,
Marston Gate.